Landscape and Literature

Landscape and Literature

THE ESSAYS OF LAWRENCE CLARK POWELL
IN THE SOUTHWEST REVIEW

Foreword by David Farmer

DEGOLYER LIBRARY
SOUTHERN METHODIST UNIVERSITY
DALLAS 1990

Table of Contents

Foreword

In the *Southwest Review* archive at DeGolyer Library is a postal card to Margaret Hartley mailed from the south of France on a spring day in 1963. It bears neither a date nor a complete postmark, although it is signed. Yet this is part of its significance and charm, for it conveys the sender's sense of rush and enthusiasm for travel. Signed "Fond regards to you and Allen—Larry," it was, of course, written by Lawrence Clark Powell.

This card's message tells us even more because it forges the link between travel and writing, landscape and literature—connections that Powell has explored with eloquence and heartfelt thoughtfulness throughout much of his career. "This is the best trip ever via Porsche; Zurich—Salzburg—Florence—Nice—& on to Spain, then France—& London for the month of May. Will do SW Rev. the best piece ever, if you like."

By 1963 Lawrence Clark Powell had been sending work to the *Southwest Review* for ten years and in that time had become a valued contributor and a good friend of its editors, Allen Maxwell and Margaret Hartley. Soon after his first recommendation to the *SWR* editors by J. Frank Dobie late in 1953, LCP worked closely with Hartley, the associate editor. Thus, with the postcard from France, Margaret Hartley knew she could expect another Powell manuscript for consideration shortly after the author returned to UCLA. Indeed, a new essay was sent on 17 September, accepted within a month, and published as "In Search of Spring" in the winter 1964 issue.

Editorial matters did not always move so swiftly, and when they slowed down, a gracious letter from Margaret Hartley would smooth the way. In a letter to LCP early in September 1955, she began: "We owe you an apology for having been so very slow in reporting to you on your essay on Jeffers, 'The Making of a Poet'.'' After explaining how summer vacations had upset the review process, she expressed her delight in this contribution, accepted it, made some deft suggestions to "change the material over a little more thoroughly into essay form," and then closed: "We hope that our delight in the essay will perhaps in some measure compensate for our delay in letting you know about it."

Four days later, Powell wrote on 13 September: "Dear Miss Hartley—You write a heart-warming letter of acceptance. Of course I don't mind the delay, and I am grateful to you for . . . anything . . . that will improve it." After offering an essay on New Mexico, "a personal impression of the land after a revisit in July," Powell ends with his warm thanks "for that precious thing a writer must have if he is to write—encouragement."

Encouragement was the touchstone for the emerging relationship between editor and author, naturally more formal at first, then growing more comfortable with the passage of time. Before long, LCP began sending Margaret Hartley some of his other publications, including the splendid Southwest Broadsides printed between 1953 and 1958, to which she responded with appropriate and keenly observant words of thanks.

Through correspondence Powell shared news not only of his travels and writing, but also of other professional milestones such as the founding of the Graduate School of Library Science at UCLA in 1959, his early retirement in 1966 after nearly thirty years of service at UCLA, and his move to Arizona to teach, consult, and, of course, to write in his so-called retirement.

In some of his letters LCP would enclose news releases relating to his activities. For example, he wrote in January 1959: "I got my library school, as per the enclosed—& will serve as dean, gradually giving up library administration in favor of teaching. Hope to have fall semester on leave & to be in Europe again, buying and writing. May I do *SWR* another travel piece?" In the same letter he asks Margaret Hartley if she received another of his books. "You did get *A Passion for*

Books from World, I trust. It has sold 2000 of 4000 copies. Amazing! I have been such a long time 'arriving'."

News of a more private nature came in February 1964 when LCP wrote "Now I'm pointing toward retirement at 60. Will be 58 this year—after 29 years at UCLA—& will write & travel & read & just sit. This is still confidential."

The death of J. Frank Dobie in 1964 touched Margaret Hartley and Lawrence Clark Powell deeply, not only because he was a treasured friend, but also because his work had influenced each of them greatly. After learning of Dobie's passing, Powell wrote: "Dear Margaret, tonight I read through my 10-year file of letters from Frank Dobie and I was between smiles and tears. I'm just beginning to realize he's gone."

Hartley replied: "If there is anyone on whom Dobie's mantle has fallen, I think it is you. Your feeling for the Southwest differs from his, of course, as your two personalities differ. But you are unquestionably the one whose sensitivity matches his."

The following year, when Margaret Hartley was named editor of the *Southwest Review*, she turned to Powell precisely for this sensitivity. In January 1965 she wrote:

"Larry, there is no friend of the magazine whom I value as highly as I do you. I still feel as I did when I wrote you a good while ago about the relationship between you and Dobie and the literary life of the Southwest. I need your help and counsel, as well as your writing, very much. And I should like to ask you to let me put your name on the masthead as one of our contributing editors. I want to reestablish such a group. . . . Now, will you do this for your cousin who is undertaking a formidable responsibility? It won't mean any added chores for you, beyond what you have done for us during our happy association these past years. It will simply make your interest official, and your consent to this will add greatly to my confidence in undertaking the editorship."

Powell's response was prompt and to the point: "I rejoice in your elevation to the editorship, and I would deem it an honor to have my name shown as contributing editor. No one can ever fill Dobie's moccasins. I'll do the best I can to be helpful.''

Over time, Lawrence Clark Powell fulfilled a number of roles with the *Southwest Review* and SMU. His essays that make up the present volume form his most sustained written contributions. In addition, he wrote occasional book reviews and submitted some of his own books for review (one written by J. Frank Dobie, others by Margaret Hartley). Beyond this Powell consulted with the DeGolyer Foundation on the placement of its great Western Americana library, and he served on the SMU Board of Publications at the invitation of President Willis Tate. Then, in 1987, when the DeGolyer Medal was created by the DeGolyer Library and the Friends of the SMU Libraries, Lawrence Clark Powell was named its first recipient. At the occasion of its presentation, he delivered a talk, ''Return to the Heartland,'' subsequently published as DeGolyer Library Keepsake #2.

Lawrence Clark Powell's association with the *Southwest Review* and SMU has extended over a span of 36 years when we consider his 1987 lecture and award and now this volume with an introduction he has just written. His eighteen-year term on the editorial board of the *SWR* ended in 1983 shortly after Margaret Hartley's death. Only a year earlier Allen Maxwell and Margaret Hartley had retired after distinguished careers with the SMU Press and the *Southwest Review* of 37 and 35 years respectively.

Naturally, LCP was sent a notice of their retirement and an invitation to a party in their honor, to which he replied: ''Tis the end of an era when you two retire! I've had no better friends of my work than you. . . . Wish I could be at the Whaleys on May 1.''

Now, to help mark the 75th anniversary of the *Southwest Review*, we offer this volume of essays written by Lawrence Clark Powell and first published in the *SWR*. They not only provide excellent examples of what this accomplished reader/observer/librarian/writer produced, these writings are also a testament to his long association with this university. Powell's contributions are a significant part of the history of a journal that had its roots in the Southwest and sought to document the voice, spirit, and mind of a region all the more complex because of the diverse historical and cultural forces that shaped it.

The archive of the *Southwest Review* illuminates how well the magazine identified, gathered, edited, and published the best writings within its scope and mission. A microcosm of this process is found in approximately one hundred and fifty letters, postcards, and telegrams exchanged between Margaret Hartley and Lawrence Clark Powell that cover a span of 29 years. The process of encouragement and adjustment between editor and author is not all these letters clarify. They also reveal the emergence of mutual respect, deep trust, and a lasting friendship.

The collection of memorable essays that follows is the result of such an association. They engage the reader because they speak to the mind as well as to the heart. For this reason Lawrence Clark Powell's writing has lasting power, which is what Margaret Hartley nourished from his first manuscript, recommended by Dobie, to his last *SWR* contribution on the subject of another of his many good friends, Henry Miller.

DAVID FARMER
DeGolyer Library
October 1990

Introduction

In twenty-eight years at UCLA writing did not earn much money. Why did I persist? A need for the attention and approval library work was not giving me. "You work so hard after hours," Fay once said, "and never get anything for it." It was obvious only to me that I was investing in a reputation that someday would pay dividends. My writing was never on company time. Thanks to her we made it, and I became known for talks on books and reading. A book on Jeffers and bibliographical work on Steinbeck were good topics.

My debut was at a college and university library group, meeting at Scripps College. It was called "Notes on Reading." When I sent it to the *California Library Association Bulletin*, it was rejected as being more literary than library. I then tried the *Wilson Library Bulletin,* where it appeared as "I Read What I Like."

That seemed more aggressive than I really was, yet it met with approval and an offer to write a column for $15.00 a month. That was more than my pride would take, although it was tempting. After five years at UCLA my pay had risen to $155.00 a month.

Occasional publication was all I had the energy for, and yet I somehow became a regular contributor to *Westways,* encouraged (and well paid) by editors from Phil Townsend Hanna to Frances Ring. By the 1950's I was also writing for *Arizona Highways* in answer to requests from its editor, Raymond Carlson, and for the *New Mexico Magazine* whose editor was George Fitzpatrick. In New York William Targ, editor of World Publishing Company, led me to write *A Passion for Books, Books in My Baggage,* and *The Little Package,* all of which went through several editions. In Los Angeles Ward Ritchie drew books from me, as did Paul Weaver at Northland Press in Flagstaff.

All of this brought me to the notice of Frances Brown, editor of the *New York Times Book Review*. In the 1950's and 1960's I wrote reviews, columns, front page pieces, all on books and reading and travel. Unusual assignments included an omnibus review of nine new encyclopedias for young people, an essay on the books I did *not* take with me on a sabbatical trip to Europe, and my choice of a paperback library for a sophisticated family. That last was syndicated in many college library periodicals.

My first appearance in the *Southwest Review* resulted from meeting J. Frank Dobie. I had given a talk to Arizona librarians which took off from his *Guide to Life and Literature of the Southwest*. He asked me to come see him. We hit it off. He suggested I submit my work to the periodical with which he had long been associated.

My first contribution was the talk I gave on Frederick Webb Hodge's 89th birthday. It is probably my favorite of all I wrote for the *SWR*, although "Revista Nueva Mexicana" comes close. It pleased me when Margaret Hartley chose the latter to end the *Southwest Review Reader,* as did her choice of Paul Horgan to open the volume. She and I did not meet many times. When editor Allen Maxwell had all he could do as director of the SMU Press, he asked Margaret to conduct our correspondence. I remember very well our first meeting which occurred without my knowing it. I was in Dallas to speak to a meeting of the Friends of the Public Library, and being early for my talk in the grand new building, I was looking at a lobby exhibit of my work. I said to a woman, also looking at the exhibit, that it was too bad it didn't include a piece to come in the *Southwest Review*, but they were taking forever to get it in print. Whereupon my fellow viewer observed quietly, "That's my fault. I'm Margaret Hartley." I suppose I blushed. At least I should have. My gaffe gave me an opening joke on myself for my talk. It was on that trip that I also met Allen.

I saw Margaret next when I returned to Dallas on a survey for the DeGolyer Foundation as to where to locate their endowed library. Mr. De stipulated in his will that it had to be in North Texas, much to the chagrin of Harry Ransom who argued that Austin was indeed in North Texas!

That was a hot summer assignment, taking me to Waco, Fort Worth, and Denton, and finally back to Dallas and a meeting with the SMU trustees, attended also by Allen Maxwell and Lon Tinkle. On day trips to the several institutions, I was able to evaluate their facilities in support of the DeGolyer benefaction. Only red carpets that week!

One evening was spent in the Public Library, near the Statler, reading in an easy chair near the main entrance and observing what comes over a person entering the heart of the whirlwind. My reading was in the latest volume of Lawrence Durrell's Alexandria Quartet. Flying home to Los Angeles I wrote "Durrell in Dallas" for the *New York Times Book Review*. That piece was reprinted by the Texas Library Association for statewide reading.

My recommendation was that the endowment be at SMU as the strongest research institution in North Texas. I saw Margaret Hartley during that survey week, and again when Fay and I returned to discuss my recommendations with the DeGolyer trustees, meeting for an opulent buffet dinner in the great book room at the hacienda, presided over by matriarchal Nell DeGolyer. It was then that I was asked to be a contributing editor to the *SWR*.

My relationship with Margaret Hartley was the ideal one of author and editor. I recognized her standards and sought to work within their guidelines. Only once did she reject a contribution, and then she was right. It did not meet the criterion of first appearance, although its modest format and limited readership in the *Robinson Jeffers Newsletter* led me to hope for an exception being made. Although I'm sure she tidied my prose and so deftly that I never knew it was done, she did not homogenize her contributors—a practice which makes some periodicals monotonous.

When in 1958 I privately printed a manuscript left by my mother upon her death, I sent *The Quiet Side of Europe* to Margaret for the pleasure I knew she would take in it. I don't know the trail she followed that led to our being Quaker cousins, but I do know that my Aunt Marian, the family's genealogist, confirmed her finding.

When Margaret Hartley left the editorship, the light went out for me. She was the review, not by anything she said or did, simply in being herself and imparting that self of knowledge, taste and skill to every issue. That's what a good editor does.

That she embraced me as a writer was my good fortune. "Remembering Henry Miller" (her title) was our last collaboration. Her review of my *California Classics* was the only review to observe that the book was as much about writing as about writers. She was a writer's editor, recognizing the ambiguous and ambivalent nature of that monster. Incidentally, Lon Tinkle saw the same thing in his review of the later *Southwest Classics*. SMU was blessed by the presence of those two critics and teachers.

I rejoice that the DeGolyer Library has recognized the importance of the *Southwest Review* by incorporating its rich archive. That I am part of it heightens my pride and joy. Dear *Southwest Review*! Dear Cousin Margaret!

LAWRENCE CLARK POWELL

Landscape and Literature

Landscape with Books

I BEGIN with the obvious question whether teaching about writing can ever penetrate to the heart of the matter. "Tell me where is Fancy bred, or in the heart or in the head?" Shakespeare asked. The origins of writing are as mysterious as those of love. "Heart" and "Head" are old-fashioned terms; "Solar Plexus" is the one D. H. Lawrence preferred.

I am less interested in the technique of writing than in the matter of character—the writer's character—and of the character of the region—the Southwest. One can choose his region; one cannot choose his character. The latter is his birthright, and is as much a part of him as the color of his hair and the shape of his nose. There are dyes for hair and there is plastic surgery for noses, but neither can alter character.

"What you are," said Emerson, "thunders so loudly as to drown out what you say." MacLeish put it somewhat differently: "A poem should not mean but be."

Although character cannot be basically changed, it can be influenced, shaped, or redirected, either for good or for bad. What are some of the forces that do this? The two principal ones are people and places. If the poet Robinson Jeffers had been forced, by one reason or another, to spend his life in his native Pittsburgh and to marry a local society woman, his poetry would have developed differently than it did from his long residence in Carmel and his marriage to a beautiful woman, an educated primitive—"more like a woman in a Scotch ballad, or a falcon," Jeffers wrote about Una; and with her death in 1950 his writing died, though he lives on in a living death.

People and places are powerful influences on a writer, and here again I am thinking in terms of character rather than of technique. What I have learned about writing from people is far less than what I have learned from writing itself. It took me four unpublished novels to learn that I am not a novelist—at least not yet; and it has taken me ten published biographies, bibliographies, and books of essays to be able to reread my prose without regret for having let it appear in print. Skin after skin have I thus shed, and if I am lucky there will be one good and life-giving book at the core of my being. I suppose this hope is what leads one to persist in writing.

Through all of this, I have had only one handbook—the dictionary —and my only class in writing came thirty years ago, in my senior year at college, in which my grade was a generous C.

Thus what I have learned from people about the art of writing has been largely from myself, by persistence and a thousand blue pencils. The chief thing I have gotten from other people, which has helped me grow as a writer, is a belief in the worth of what I was doing, and encouragement to persist.

If one hasn't this core of belief in oneself as a writer, confirmed and strengthened by friends' faith and encouragement, all the classes and craft in the world won't make that person a writer of any worth.

Thus I suppose the first thing to inquire into is one's own character, in order to find out what kind of writing should be embraced. If one isn't curious about other people, who they are and why they behave as they do, he should not try to be a novelist. If one has no flair for research, he should forego historical writing. If he cares naught for detail and accuracy, bibliography should be eschewed. If he be unemotional and prosaic, rather than lyric, poetry is not for him. And to write essays, one must be in love, with the English language, and also in awe of it—a state of being just about as rewarding, and as difficult, as loving a woman.

What about a place, a region, as a factor in the modification and development of character? How do landscapes become bookscapes?

(Landscape is in the dictionary, but not bookscape. By bookscape I mean that wedding of a writer and a region from which no divorce is possible, and which produces such literary children as *Walden, Huckleberry Finn, The Return of the Native,* and *Ulysses.*) This is a matter of mystery, of fascination, and the way to approach it is by an examination of certain southwestern books, to see if we can discover what happened. What led Zane Grey, the man from Zanesville, Ohio, from being a city dentist to the authorship of *Riders of the Purple Sage*? What happened in the life of Will Levington Comfort, who began by composing the superficial *Routledge Rides Alone* and ended by writing the profound *Apache,* the novel about Mangas Coloradas which Dobie called the most moving of all novels about the Indians of the Southwest? Why do Harvey Fergusson's New Mexican novels go on getting better the longer he lives in California, and John Steinbeck's California novels get worse, from the time he left his native state?

Character is the answer. The influence of people and places upon these writers' personalities. There is no more enthralling subject than the study of a good writer getting worse or of an average writer getting better. I am thinking of Zane Grey and Harvey Fergusson.

A teacher cannot alter a student's basic character, but he can set in motion some of the intellectual and emotional processes which will result in self-examination, inventorying of his native assets, and measurement of his own worth against masters in the field. A teacher of writing should lead the student to one of two resolutions: to become a better writer, or to give up writing.

My purpose therefore is a moral one. I believe in the essential goodness and teachability of people. I love this region we call the Southwest. I believe that there are just as many good unwritten books about the Southwest as have been written about it, that the emergence of genius is absolutely unpredictable either in time or in place, and that another Emerson or Whitman or Melville, a Hemingway, a Jeffers, or a Willa Cather may be at a school desk or playground today in Ash Fork, Snow Flake, or Roswell.

I am not a snob in my beliefs about writing. I write for money, but I take money only for writing which is the very best of which I am capable and which is the projection of my own character. I feel less pity for the prostitute writers in cribs, from Hollywood east, than I do for prostitute women. Writing for the popular market can be profitable and honest and lifesaving, if a writer has a character which can survive the perils of this alluring occupation. Ernest Haycox was such a one, and in his last work, *The Earthbreakers*, he wrote the book he'd nursed and nourished and kept alive within himself all through the potboiling years. Alan Le May is another one whose mature work, popular and successful though it be, breaks through to a new dimension.

Suppose one is determined to use the Southwest as the setting for his writing. How does he go about it? Does he have to be a native son? Not necessarily. If he is, and has lived most of his years where he was born, perhaps he should leave the Southwest. By looking back on his homeland from afar, he might achieve two things not possible when he is too close to his native habitat. I mean perspective and nostalgia. Perspective will give a better sense of form and proportion to his work. Nostalgia will intensify its emotion. From his vantage point in Berkeley, California, Harvey Fergusson looked back on his native New Mexico and wrote *Grant of Kingdom*, a story about the Maxwell Land Grant in northeastern New Mexico, which is to me one of the best of all Southwest novels.

But it is easy to disprove this thesis by citing Tom Lea's *The Wonderful Country*, written in El Paso, by a native of that town, about the border country of Texas-Chihuahua, New Mexico-Sonora, a novel which I rate with *Grant of Kingdom* among the few great novels about the Southwest.

And if one is not a native son, or a long-time resident of the Southwest, then how does he go about turning landscapes into bookscapes? It all depends on his equipment—on his sensitivity, his absorptive capacity, and creative stamina. If these qualities are highly developed, he can harbor for only a season in a locale, soak up material, move on, and write, for example, *The Silverado Squatters*, Stevenson's never surpassed account of the Napa Valley in Northern California, where he honeymooned for a month; or "The Princess," D. H. Lawrence's short story of the Sangre de Cristos, which embodies the quintessense of his genius; or come briefly to a southwestern university town, engulf the library and its staff in a prodigious feat of research, then write Elliott Arnold's *Blood Brother*.

If one's work is going to rise above the average, he is going to have to be on fire when he conceives it, and then be able to bank the fire when he writes it. To infuse a sense of excitement into prose is necessary, if that prose is going to excite readers. How is this done? Here we are back at the mysterious heart of the matter. To be excited is commonplace; to write prose which is alive and electric and communicative is rare, calling for nothing less than mastery of language.

Zane Grey felt this excitement over the southwestern setting and he got it into his first and best books—*The Heritage of the Desert*, *Riders of the Purple Sage*, and *The Rainbow Trail*; and yet his inability to avoid clichés kept his prose from having any distinction. Likewise his emotions were basically immature. These two points can be illustrated with one quotation from an article on his own career which Zane Grey wrote for the *American Magazine* in 1924:

> To my mind, romance is only another name for idealism; a glimpse through the painted windows of the dreams of youth; the spirit, not the letter, of life. We all have in our hearts the kingdom of adventure. Somewhere in the depths of every soul is the inheritance of the primitive day. I speak to that.
>
> Love also is only another name for romance. The realists write of its change and its death. But I cannot see that love ever changes or ever dies. If so, what is the use of living?
>
> So, also, the books of stark-naked realism show primitive men retrograding to the level of the brute. But my own investigation,

my reading of frontier history, my long strife to explore the lonely and hidden wilderness of the West, have proved to me that hard men of the open also climb to the heights of nobility and sacrifice, to a supreme proof of the evolution of man, to a realization of God.

It is this mawkishness which kept Zane Grey out of the first ranks of southwestern novelists. (Sales figures are no refutation, for Gene Stratton Porter and Harold Bell Wright exceeded Zane Grey in sales.)

It was this genteel tradition in romantic fiction, sired by Fenimore Cooper, Scott, and Kipling, that led Harvey Fergusson to rebellion in his first Southwest novel called *Wolf Song*. His criticism of the Romantic school was that although their stories are taken from life, as Zane Grey's were, their characters are lifeless.

This leads from setting to sex, or from landscape to love.

"Take all the pioneer women in the chronicles," J. Frank Dobie once wrote me; "not a single one of them has a breast, or a flank, or a perfume in the mouth."

If setting, its power and its beauty, is difficult to assimilate into fiction, then sex is almost impossible. To be literal is not the way to fecundate Zane Grey's sterile romanticism. Sexual literalism is disgusting or, worse, boring. To write of sexual excitement and tension, of the strength and the tenderness which are the twin sides of the deepest sexual experience, and of its transforming effect on the participants—this is an art rarely mastered by writers. When I say that it too is a matter of character, I do not necessarily mean of autobiography.

In *Death Comes for the Archbishop* Willa Cather did not have to meet the problem, for her ecclesiastical characters had sublimated sexual emotions through service and sacrifice. Comfort's heroic *Apache* is also on a super-sexual level. *Blood Brother* would have achieved greater stature if its author had not been moved by various reasons to invent a romance between Tom Jeffords and an Apache princess.

A successful novel need not have sexual elements, but if a novel is written with sex as one of the forces which move its characters, then artful skill is called for to keep the theme from the extremes of either Zane Grey or Mickey Spillane.

A good model is Harvey Fergusson. His treatment of sexual experience is frank, detailed only to a point, strong, and tender; and profoundly true to the emotions of a man and a woman preceding and following the act of love. To portray the mounting tension and the following relaxation—what men and women feel and say and do before, during, and after love—calls for deep insight into emotion and firm control over language. From *Wolf Song* through *The Life of Riley* to *Grant of Kingdom* and *The Conquest of Don Pedro*, Harvey Fergusson has demonstrated a twin mastery of love and landscape.

Frank Waters is another southwestern writer with unusual skill in these matters. His novel, *People of the Valley*, is laid in the Guadalupita Valley above Mora, and is as true to the landscape of that lovely place as it is to the changing love life of Maria, its heroine, in her development from a shy goat girl through sensual womanhood to the witchcrafty old Maria della Valle, the rich and powerful ruler of the region who would not be displaced by a government dam.

And so, finally, here is the wide and wonderful Southwest as a potential setting for writing—lots of landscape, more and more people seeking wealth or health or safety from cities, an arid region with a fabled history from Onate to Oppenheimer, deep canyoned, high mountained, watered by the Rio Grande, the Pecos, the Verde, and the Colorado, traversed by trains of silvery beauty, transcended by distance-devouring airplanes, an ocean-like land with many islands of refuge and refreshment, solace and strength (I mean libraries and churches), peopled by strong men, fair women, wise elders, and children, of many races, a land of colored earth and cloudy skies, more real than any paradise hereafter.

If a writer would transform these landscapes with people into landscapes with books, he must sink roots into its sandy soil, send up feelers into its clear air. He must try to think clearly, to feel deeply, to write honestly. If he is fortunate, he will make a living, but his work will never be any more essentially clear and deep and honest than he himself is, and he will be judged finally not for how many copies his books have sold, but for what they have done to enrich the lives of their readers, now and in time to come.

Sky, Sun & Water:
The Southwest of Frederick Webb Hodge

S KY, sun, and water. These are not obscure terms. The sky is overhead, is blue or black, is clouded or starry. The sun rises, sets, is warmth, is life. And water is wet, flows, and also is life, and causes trouble between Arizona and California.

The Southwest. Now there is a term which does not mean the same thing to all people. How far Northeast does the Southwest start? Texans issue a journal called the *Southwestern Historical Quarterly* which is pure Texas. There is a Southwestern Library Association which includes Louisiana and not California. The "Southwestern Historical Series," published by Arthur Clark of Glendale, covers Missouri, Arkansas, and Colorado. The Rockefeller Foundation has set up two Southwest research programs, one at the Huntington Library which includes Utah, and the other at Norman which takes in Oklahoma and Texas.

There are reasons of land and of weather, of history and of culture for including these various states and regions in the Southwest, none of which I shall deny. My intention is, however, to be somewhat narrower, and for two reasons: first, my own experience in the Southwest has been limited; and second, Frederick Webb Hodge has worked chiefly within the same limits. So then New Mexico, Arizona, and southwestern California are the Southwest of my sky, sun, and water.

How best approach this region? What words to use? How brighten its shadow, soften its dazzle? It is such an ancient region. Two of its states were named even before the New England colonies were founded. Since the Middle Ages, Indians, Spaniards, and gringos have been coming and going, eating, loving, and fighting, leaving cultural traces; and since Adolf Bandelier, Washington Mathews, and Frank Cushing began their field studies in the 1880's, scientists have been working in field and library, founding museums, publishing monographs and magazines, so that there is little pioneer work left to be done. The pueblos have even been photographed from the air, and all the roads mapped if not paved. Few are the places on the charts which still read "wilderness area," and such primitive regions as Cochise's Stronghold and Monument Valley have suffered the ultimate indignity of serving as locations for movie companies from Hollywood.

A negative approach to this Southwest would be my lack of any deep bibliographical interest in the region. The earliest imprints of New Mexico, Arizona, and Southern California do not excite me. Neither am I a historian. Although I know that Cabeza de Vaca came first, I am unable to name his followers in their proper order: Coronado, Vargas, Oñate, Mogollon, Alvarado, Armijo, Anza and Kino, Marcos de Niza—the music of their names is quite enough for me. Nor am I anthropologist, archeologist, ethnologist, meteorologist, geologist, or geographer. I am a mere librarian, a bookkeeper, yet fitted with a restless foot and a roving eye, and a desire to leave a few written testaments to posterity.

Throughout my forty-seven years I have been crisscrossing this Southwest, first as a babe in arms, then as an excited boy on the California Limited, giving handouts to hoboes riding blind baggage; and later as a hitchhiker and a driver, and finally as a belted passenger by plane. I have never roughed it in this region, nor ridden a horse for more than a few feet: and although I know that I shall sleep at last on the hard bed of earth, as long as there remains a bit of flesh on my bones I prefer a feather bed at night.

Sure, I'm a city dude, yet with an increasing dislike for what is happening to my home city of Los Angeles. Here we have plenty of water, but diminishing sky and sun, with the result that I have found myself ineluctably drawn by the land beyond the River, where there is little water and much sky and sun. One cannot live by water alone.

Last September I made a journey by air, via San Diego, Yuma, and Phoenix to Albuquerque, where I hired a car and drove a thousand miles through that Land of Enchantment; and everywhere I went on that trip, by air and land, on wheel and foot, I felt the presence at my side of Frederick Webb Hodge, my colleague who was born long ago in 1864, and far away at Plymouth, England. Before starting my trip I called on him at the Southwest Museum and asked if he could recall what it was that had first bound him to the Southwest. His answer was unhesitating.

"I remember very well what it was," he said. "I got off the train at Fort Wingate and took a deep breath. It was sage I smelled: *artemesia tridentata*. And then I looked at the landscape. I had never seen such clear air. That was it: the good smell and the pure air."

"Do you remember when that was?" I asked.

"Of course I do," he replied. "It was in 1886 and I was not quite twenty-two."

The plane crossed the Colorado at Yuma, and I looked down on the confluence of the Colorado and the Gila, and on the All-American Canal flowing on a concrete bed through thirsty sand. The Salton Sea was visible to the north. Everywhere an immense thirstiness of land under a thirsty sun and sky. Seen from ten thousand feet the River at Yuma looks peaceful and relaxed, its long flow nearly ended, the final tributary gathered in, soon to lose itself in the salty Gulf.

Here again my mind turned to Hodge, for Yuma evoked Garces, and the martyred priest recalled Hodge's footnotes to Coues' edition of Garces' *Journal*, published in 1900. These topographical notes which serve to pinpoint Garces on the map are good reading. They are not merely topographical notes, but often miniature essays akin to the entries in Hodge's great *Handbook of the American Indians*, as for example this one which comments on Garces' statement that the Indians kissed the Spaniards' hands:

It is extremely doubtful if the natives actually kissed the hands of the Spaniards; more probably, as a greeting of friendship inspired by religious fervor, the Indian grasped the hand of the priest, drew it toward his own mouth, inhaled from it the "breath of life," and then passed the clasped hands toward the mouth of the Spaniard, who was supposed to do the same. This custom, which is still common among the Zuñis at least, may be regarded rather as religious greeting than as a mere gesture of courtesy.

I must confess that *where* Garces went interests me less than *who* Garces was. The force of religious zeal that moved this Franciscan to bitter hardship and ultimate martyrdom is the lasting thing, and in all my reading about the Southwest I have sought to pass beyond bibliographical points and topographical itineraries, and seek the spirit that moved men to such heroism and sacrifice. It is customary now for motorists in summer to cross the Mojave Desert by dark in order to avoid the heat. Francisco Garces crisscrossed this region on foot at all seasons. He was a man.

My interest in him began twenty years ago in the stoneyard of a Los Angeles sculptor. This friend was the supervisor of WPA projects in Southern California, and one morning a draying company delivered to his yard an enormous block of limestone from the harbor. It had come all the way from France by water, and was of particular interest to me because it had been quarried in the Côte d'Or near Dijon, that golden land whence comes the limestone of Burgundy, soft and easy to work when first cut, and hardening upon exposure to air.

There I watched it gradually shaped by another sculptor into the great figure of Garces which now graces the traffic circle in Bakersfield, the most beautiful western monument known to me. It stands there because Garces was the discoverer of the lower San Joaquin Valley. There is also a statue of him in Yuma at the Mission School,

on the site of his martyrdom by the Indians in 1781, a more conventional treatment of the Padre blessing the Indians, and lacking the
simple nobility of the Kern County figure.

There is also a novel about Garces which illuminates his life more
than any biography yet set down. Written by Helen White, it is called
Dust on the King's Highway. An inspired work of fiction about a man
is more essentially truthful than a pedestrian work of fact, and this
novel tells me more of what must have moved these pioneer priests
than all the conventional treatises I have ever read. Here is how Miss
White describes the martyrdom of Garces:

> Again, he heard the clubs whistle through the air, and again
> the sea of flame burst over his body and rose above his head.
> And in a mighty agony the spirit thrashed that it might not be
> completely engulfed in the body's foundering. And then above
> the pain there shot up like a hand above a sinking head, a sharp
> spear of consciousness, and he cried out, "My Lord!" and then
> he knew with a great clarity that this time the words did not
> matter. For He would understand.
>
> Again, the clubs swung and fell, but this time Garces made
> no effort to get up. For he did not hear their gleaming hiss, and
> the heavy crash of their fall. He was listening to a bell ringing out
> from a great height, ringing up and down the rivers, ringing
> the joyous words of the *Magnificat*, "My soul doth magnify the
> Lord!" And high above the dusty brush of the river bottom, he
> saw the shining highway stretch, and he saw a host of men,
> women, and children down the broad way, white and brown,
> Indian and Spanish, the living and the dead alike, and they were
> singing the triumphant words to the measured sweetness of the
> bell.

Flying up the Gila to its confluence with the Salado, the Salt, at
Phoenix, I found myself obsessed by thoughts of water (the river was

dry and they had served ham for lunch) and depressed by the pro-
liferation of Arizona's capital city, which Erna Fergusson called "the
desert converted into California." It was thereabouts that Hodge's
first excavating was done, back in 1886 when he first came to New
Mexico and Arizona with the Hemenway expedition. When I asked
Hodge what he remembered best of that adventure, he said jokingly
that it was the water he drank from the Hassayampa, that fabled
tributary of the Gila whose waters are said to make one's speech
super-factual.

If the Central Arizona Project is approved and Colorado River
water is hoisted and boosted and brought to the Salt River Valley,
God help the Phoenicians! Agriculture will be followed by industry,
even as in Southern California, and the refugees from smog who have
fled Los Angeles to Phoenix will have once again to trek over the
mountains, this time to New Mexico; and the forced flow of water
uphill from Phoenix to Tucson will mean that the two cities ulti-
mately become one, even as Los Angeles and San Diego are doomed
eventually to meet and to merge.

Flying from Phoenix to Albuquerque above the great open-pit
copper mine at Morenci, its tailings pistachio-colored, and over the
mountain stronghold of the White River Apache, I listed the novels
I would recommend to one who wanted the essence of the Southwest with a minimum of reading. There would be Bandelier's *The
Delight Makers*, first of all Southwest novels, by the anthropologist
who pioneered southwestern field work and inspired Hodge, Lummis,
Bolton, and many another. Bandelier believed that the truths of ethnology could be presented to the general public best by means of
fiction; his novel deserves reprinting for its faithful picture of pueblo
life. La Farge's *Laughing Boy*, Will Comfort's *Apache*, Corle's *Fig
Tree John*, Cather's *Death Comes for the Archbishop*, and the New Mexican series of Rio Grande novels by Harvey Fergusson are true to life
as much nonfiction about the Southwest is not. This has been recognized by Hodge, in tributes he has paid to the Apache novels by
Comfort and Corle.

In a lifetime of reading I have gutted many a book about this region, hungering for facts and then for the power of language which makes facts flower and statistics sing. Lummis' books are often factually satisfying. His *Mesa, Cañon and Pueblo* is one of the best of all books about the Southwest, in the amount of information it contains. Don Carlos' prose, however, is often as rough as his personality. Neither man nor style ever mellowed. Yet he was one of our great creative men, and such men can be forgiven a few minor imperfections.

If I had to choose a single nonfiction work about the Southwest, it would be a book I first read after my September journey. It is a good sequel to the author's California classic, *The Land of Little Rain*. Mary Austin's *Land of Journeys' Ending* has facts of places and people, of history and myth, and it also has overtones of feeling and beauty which the Southwest stirs in sensitive beholders. In this book Mary Austin's personality is subordinate to the Southwest, which is rarely true of Lummis, and her style and rhythm are wedded to her subject. Here is an example of what I mean:

> To many people grass is as indispensable an index of fertility in the earth as long hair is of femininity in a woman. Actually, all that grass and other annual cover afford to the casual observer, is evidence of the quick, continuous rhythms of vegetating life. But in arid regions where the period of growth is confined to the short season of maximum rainfall, the processes of foliation and floration are pushed almost to explosion; followed by a long quiescence in which life merely persists.

When Mary Austin came to Los Angeles from Inyo at the turn of the century and was drawn into the Lummis circle, it was not Lummis who molded her, it was Hodge. She recalls the meeting in *Earth Horizon*:

> There was the man she wanted most to meet, Dr. Frederick Webb Hodge, the Indian specialist, who told her the thing she

wanted most to know, the way of collecting and recording Indian affairs. "Let be," he said, "the strange and unusual; fix on the usual, the thing that is always done, the way of the tribe; the way of the average; the way and the why of it." She was young enough to be told, and Dr. Hodge was authority enough to be accepted as telling. The way and the why; it remained with her and colored the whole of her interest in tribal affairs. It was the beginning of an influence that lasted out her life, a way of reference, a contingent.

The Arizona chapters of this book are on the Papagueria—the region south of Tucson where the Papago Indians, called the Bean People, have their abode—on the cactus forests around Tucson, on the Rio Colorado and Boboquivari, sacred mountain of the Papagos. Hers is a romantic view of the Southwest. "By land," she writes, "I mean all those things common to a given region: the flow of prevailing winds, the succession of vegetal cover, the legend of ancient life; and the scene, above everything the magnificently shaped and colored scene."

From Albuquerque I journeyed by car up the Rio Grande to Santa Fe and Taos, drawn by the prospect of an *entrada* into Colorado and a return to the Mesa Verde, where years ago I sensed what Mary Austin calls "the residue of personality that man leaves in all places once frequented." I trudged the dusty way from Taos town to Taos pueblo, pausing en route to watch an Indian raking mown alfalfa and to hear him sing a harvest song—lonely, happy, immemorial music of the earth. Inside the pueblo I dodged Texan motorists and found haven on the great log bridge over the creek. Cool flow of water under a fierce sun and sky of cobalt, sky of turquoise, New Mexican sky of a blue like no other, crystalline blue and cloud-capped, there at the alluvial base of the Sangre de Cristos, my pocket full of wild plums gathered along the way, a puckery fruit that is better made into jelly than eaten raw.

In Santa Fe the only call I made was on Haniel Long—to receive for the UCLA Library the original manuscripts of his two beautiful books on Cabeza de Vaca and Malinche, Cortes' Indian friend. At the Cathedral I paid homage to the statue of Lamy which inspired Willa Cather's *Archbishop*. And then I headed southwest, nearly back to Arizona, to the self-styled Indian capital of Gallup. A few miles east of the town I paused where the road turns off to Fort Wingate, now an ordnance depot, and saw what Hodge saw sixty-seven years ago when he first saw the Southwest. Time passes, Hodge and the earth remain, and that particular piece of New Mexican earth, lying exposed on the grassy windswept plateau running west from the Divide, between salmon-colored sandstone cliffs on the north and dark cedar-covered hills on the south.

In Gallup I felt a pull to journey ninety-four miles north to Shiprock, the great basalt plug sacred to the Navaho. The pull to Zuñi was stronger, for Hodge too was drawing me to the region where two of his most important missions were accomplished.

But first I spent an evening in Gallup, doing what I often did on lonely nights in Dijon twenty years ago, watching the trains pass through the station. First came the westbound Chief, followed by the Grand Canyon, two sections of the California Limited, El Capitan, and then the Super Chief, all running closely together, stopping only long enough to water the diesels, and finally to allow an eastbound freight to clear the yards and gather speed toward the Divide.

I am not one of those who bemoan the passing of the steam locomotive. The Santa Fe's diesel fleet—its passenger engines painted red and yellow, its freight engines blue and yellow—pleases me by its trim and powerful beauty. Standing there on the platform I recited the litany of Pullman car names as they passed. Coconino Princess, Pinos Altos, Mimbres Gap, Blue Mesa, Eagle Nest, Red River Valley —and a lone New York Central car, crow among swans, named Taylors Falls. Window shades were drawn. Few passengers alighted. A woman walked her poodle. The California Limited included two Horse Express cars loaded with racers for Santa Anita, each car carrying also a mascot dog and a groom, one of whom looked more like a girl than a boy.

Early next morning I drove the forty miles to Zuñi, where from the sunbaked pueblo's post office I mailed a card to Hodge, an adopted Zuñi, addressing him by his tribal name, Teluli, which means "Dig Your Cellar."

Dig he did, in the early twenties, to excavate the nearby pueblo of Hawikuh, the history of which ancient city of Cíbola Hodge has told in a volume printed in 1937 by Ward Ritchie. Here it was that Marcos de Niza came in 1539, with the virile Barbary Negro named Estévan (he of the parrot feathers and rattling gourds who had been with Cabeza de Vaca, and also with too many Indian women for his own good—he was murdered by the Zuñis of Hawikuh). Here the great Spanish influx had concentrated, seeking the gold and turquoise of the Seven Golden Cities of Cíbola.

It was in Hodge's volume on Hawikuh that I first saw pictures of my next destination, soft collotype plates of the great rock called by the Spaniards El Morro and by the Americans Inscription Rock, formed of buff-colored Navajo sandstone, capped with a stratum of the red Dakota stone. In working on Philosopher Pickett a dozen years ago I had come across his friends the Kern brothers, and learned that it was Richard Kern who first copied the inscriptions while serving as artist with the Simpson expedition into the Navajo country. Here is Lieutenant Simpson's report of his discovery of El Morro —the first description of it in English:

A couple of miles further, meeting in the road Mr. Lewis, who was waiting for me to offer his services as guide to a rock upon the face of which were, according to his repeated assertions, half an acre of inscriptions, many of them very beautiful,

and upon its summit some ruins of a very extraordinary character, I at once fell in with the project, and obtained from the
colonel commanding the necessary permission. Taking with me
one of my assistants, Mr. R. H. Kern, ever zealous in an enter-
prise of this kind; the faithful Bird, an *employé* who had been
with me ever since I left Fort Smith, we diverged from the
command. . . with the expectation of not again meeting it until
we should reach the Pueblo of Laguna, from seventy to eighty
miles distant. There were many in the command who were
inclined to the belief that Lewis's representations were all gam-
mon. In regard to the *extent* of the inscriptions, I could not but
believe so too ; but as respects the fact of there being some toler-
able basis for so grandiloquent a description, I could not, rea-
soning upon general principles of human nature, reject it. Mr.
Lewis had been a trader among the Navajos, and, according to
his statement, had seen these inscriptions in his journeyings to
and from their country. And now he was ready to conduct me
to the spot. How could I doubt his sincerity? I could not; and
my faith was rewarded by the result.

Bearing off slightly to the right from the route of the troops,
we traversed for eight miles a country varied, in places, by low
mesas, blackened along their crests by outcrops of basalt, and
on our left by fantastic white and red sandstone rocks, some of
them looking like steamboats, and others presenting very much
the appearance of facades of heavy Egyptian architecture. This
distance traversed, we came to a quadrangular mass of sandstone
rock, of a pearly whitish aspect, from two hundred to two hundred and fifty feet in height, and strikingly peculiar on account
of its massive character and the Egyptian style of its natural
buttresses and domes. . . .

Skirting this stupendous mass of rock, on its left or north
side, for about a mile, the guide, just as we had reached its
eastern terminus, was noticed to leave us, and ascend a low

mound or ramp at its base, the better, as it appeared, to scan the face of the rock, which he had scarcely reached before he cried out to us to come up. We immediately went up, and, sure enough, here were inscriptions, and some of them very beautiful; and, although, with those which we afterwards examined on the south face of the rock, there could not be said to be half an acre of them, yet the hyperbole was not near as extravagant as I was prepared to find it. The fact then being certain that here were indeed inscriptions of interest, if not value, one of them dating as far back as 1605, all of them very ancient, and several of them very deeply as well as beautifully engraven, I gave directions for a halt—Bird at once proceeding to get up a meal, and Mr. Kern and myself to the work of making facsimiles of the inscriptions.

None of this had prepared me for the actual experience which befell me that morning after I left Zuñi pueblo and followed the road east, past Corn Mountain, sacred haunt of the thunderbird, and on between the cedar-wooded, red-banded mesas, still just as the good lieutenant described them; the road deserted except for an occasional pickup truck of the Indians, met and passed in a rousing cloud of red dust. Except for a single ranger, the national monument was deserted. This man was a cordial Texan (albeit a marginal Texan, having been born in El Paso) who guided me around the base of the Rock where the inscriptions are, past the natural cistern which for centuries made the Rock the stopping place for travelers between Zuñi and Ácoma. I deciphered the very first inscription of all, dated 1605, and it moved me more deeply than all the inscriptions in Westminster Abbey.

> *Pasó por aqui el adelantado Don Juan de Oñate*
> *del descubrimento de la Mar del Sur*
> *el diez y seis de abril de mil seiscientos cinco.*

Then the ranger left me to climb the Rock alone, and I made my way around to the west face, past the inscription which read "Lieut.

J. H. Simpson, U.S.A. and R. H. Kern, artist, visited and copied these inscriptions, September 17th and 18th, 1849." It was only two years later that Kern was murdered by the Utes.

Look out for rattlesnakes, the ranger warned me, but I saw none as I climbed the switchback trail to the rocky top of El Morro, where the path is marked by stone cairns. I came to the edge of the cleft that penetrates the Rock from the south, a deep *rincón* with pines and grassy floor, a perfect ceremonial stage for the Zuñis who once inhabited the mesa top. I rested awhile before making the descent down the east face by trail and ladder, and saw a flock of sheep flow past the base of the Rock eastward toward Ácoma. An Indian boy and two dogs were herding the beasts. Like water they flowed, dammed up momentarily as the bellwether stopped to graze, then spilled over in a gray flood, irresistible as a breaking wave. Blue sky, smell of sun-warmed pines, a mewing eagle disturbed by my invasion of his realm, wild cry of shepherd, bark of dogs, and ring of bell—every cell in my body responded in that moment of union with my environment.

Mary Austin has a beautiful chapter on El Morro; its final paragraph expresses the mystical experience I had there on that September morning, akin to the one I had years before on the Mesa Verde:

Here I shall haunt, and as the time-streams bend and swirl about the Rock, I shall see again all the times that I have loved, and know certainly all that now I guess at. I shall hear the drums far down in the dancing-place, and talk with feather-vendors going up to Chaco and the cliff dwellings of Cañon de Chelly....

I shall see the Fire Dance on the top of Toyoallanne, and know what was in the hearts of the men of Pecos when they came down to Hawikuh in 1540. You, of a hundred years from now, if when you visit the Rock, you see the cupped silken wings of the argemone burst and float apart when there is no wind; or if, when all around is still, a sudden stir in the short-leaved pines, or fresh eagle feathers blown upon the shrine, that will be I making known in such fashion as I may the land's undying quality.

Back at the ranger's station, I found him working at his desk, and I asked him how one went about getting a job like his.

"You have to take a civil service exam," he said. "And before that it's best to have had some range experience." He eyed me critically, a little puzzled by my garb of levis, flannel shirt, and sailor hat. "What would be your line?" he asked.

"I'm a writer," I said.

"So am I!" he snorted, pointing to the papers on his desk. "Forms, paper work, questionnaires. Now they want to know how many visitors we expect in the next ten years and if the water supply is adequate for this X-number. It gets worse every year. I voted the other way last time, but now the paper work is heavier than ever."

The road went eastward over the Divide, north to Grants on the highway, then southeast to Ácoma, oldest continuously inhabited village in America. Here also I found the tourist wave subsided, and the men of the pueblo at work repairing the roof of the church. As I climbed the rock trail by crevice and ladder, I heard the rhythmic cry of men toiling in unison, and when I gained the summit, I saw a great sight. A hundred men or more, some on the roof of the church and some at the base of the wall, were hauling up by rope and pulley forty-foot pine logs to serve as new rafters. They were between hauls as I came on the scene, planning the next operation in a hubbub of commands and counter-commands, the rooftoppers roaring directions to the groundlings, most of whom were squatting in the shade of the wall. Order finally prevailed, as the ropes were secured and the next log began to roll slowly up the wall toward the roof.

Hola! cried the leader, and *Hola!* responded the men with a great pull on the ropes. The inevitable joker spotted me watching from the shade, and trotted over to put an end of rope in my hands. "Everybody work here!" he grunted. The men laughed and I felt a part of the group, albeit a butt end.

Nearer and nearer the long log came to the top, and as it finally rolled over onto the roof the long line of heads disappeared with it, then popped up again like so many jacks-in-a-box, with a single hoarse cry of "Agua! Agua!"

Within the church of St. Stephen I prayed in silence to the muted cries of the next hauling, and I recalled a story Fred Hodge told me of a Palm Sunday ceremony he had witnessed in that very church, half a century ago. There were no palms, of course, and the worshippers came up the aisles in a long procession, bearing cedar boughs which they had decorated with bright paper cutouts and placards. Lastly there came one small Ácoman, under a large juniper crowned with a red and white poster which read, "Treat yourself to the best: Chew Mail Pouch."

I left the sky pueblo by the sand trail, starting out at a slow walk and gathering speed down the steep descent, until finally I was going at a dead run, unable to halt before I reached the bottom, where I drank a tepid Coca-Cola and bought a postcard from two Ácoman squaws.

The time was now midafternoon and I had one more stop before returning to Albuquerque for the night. My destination had been visible from the top of Ácoma, a larger mesa three miles to the north. But not just another mesa; it was the mesa called by the Indians Katsímo and by the Spaniards La Mesa Encantada. It was there that Hodge performed one of the most brilliant feats of his career. One of Lummis' first books contained the legend of Katsímo; of how it was said ages ago to have been inhabited by the Ácomans, and one day when the village descended to work in the fields a great storm destroyed the rock trail back to the mesa summit and the Indians were unable to regain the top. Three women left on high starved to death—whence came the legend of the Enchanted Mesa.

A Princeton archeologist named Libbey took exception to Lummis' story and in the 1890's came west to disprove it—as he said, to disenchant the mesa. After four days of preparation, equipped with a lifesaving gun which shot a line over the mesa, he had himself hauled to the top in a bosun's chair. A quick reconnaissance convinced him that his was the first human foot ever to tread the top, and his telegraphed story made a splash in the New York papers. Whereupon Lummis invited Hodge, then with the United States Bureau of Ethnology, to verify his belief that the Enchanted Mesa had once been a pueblo site.

Accompanied by a small party, including the bookselling photographer A. C. Vroman, Hodge gained the mesa top in a matter of hours, camped there for two days, and found enough evidence of former habitation to bury Professor Libbey deeply and forever. Illustrated with Vroman's magnificent photographs, Hodge's story appeared in *Century* magazine, *Harper's*, and *Land of Sunshine*, while Lummis beat a steady tattoo on the poor Princetonian's hide. Here is an example of what Don Carlos did to Libbey, with only his pen as a weapon:

> To the stranger it may seem remarkable that such mistakes could be made as those of the ''disenchantment''; yet we should not be puzzled if ever so intelligent a man who had never looked into a chemistry laboratory were to blunder in attempting a difficult assay. If there is an esoteric subject on earth it is Southwestern archaeology. The very meteorology and landscapes are recondite to the man from humid lands. The people who make shipwreck here in mines, ranching, cattle, are precisely those who know all about those things before they come, and in ethnology no less. The most extraordinary genius that was ever bent upon our archaeology needed eleven years of monumental study and of real hardship to learn what Bandelier learned of New Mexico. He lived as an Indian among Indians, trudged on foot thousands of desert miles, lay alone in the snow with smallpox, and braved innumerable other things that he might know. Dr. Mathews began a work he would not yet call finished while

many of his successors were still school-boys. Mr. Cushing bore
years of deprivation before even his most rare talent as an ar-
chaeologic detective made him an authority on the Southwest.
Mr. Hodge, whose patient, prudent, competent work has gained
him substantial reputation wherever there are scientists, earned
it by years of arduous experience in the field, on top of all the
study required. In New Mexico, as elsewhere—and much more
pointedly than in some other fields—the only way to know is to
have learned.

Now I wanted to see for myself the top of the Enchanted Mesa.
The ranger in charge of Ácoma Reservation said it was not a safe
climb for a single person. First there was a talus slope to scramble up,
then a smooth rock face with toe holds leading to a crevice ladder,
and finally a parapet to be surmounted. By the time I reached the
smooth area the sandstone was a radiant heater, and I sat in the shade
of a juniper bush, content to take Hodge's word that the mesa had
once been inhabited.

Ah, but it was peaceful there, with only a dove, a lizard, and a
butterfly for company. The juniper berries were green and purple,
while beneath me a ripe field of grama grass led to Ácoma, its dwellings barely distinguishable from the rock. Blue sky, hot sun, and flow
of water dammed into a shining pond, a few grazing horses, and no
visible humans. Far to the north dark curtains of rain dropped from
heaven to earth. This was journey's end; the rest would be anti-
climax.

Presently I roused myself and carved my rubric in the soft rock:
Pasó por aqui. . .

Sky, sun, and water, the Southwest and Fred Hodge.
   These are the immortal elements.
      This is the region we inhabit.
      Here is the man we honor and love.

Revista Nueva Mexicana

S EEK essences, enduring things, touchstones, and symbols; try to recreate in prose what makes this country so increasingly meaningful and necessary to one. Altitude, distance, color, configuration, history, and culture—in them dwell the essential things, but they must be extracted. ''Crack the rock if so you list, bring to light the amethyst.'' Costs nothing to try. Some have succeeded—Lummis, Lawrence, Long, La Farge, Horgan, Waters, the Fergussons—proving that it is possible. Stand books on the shelf, hang up maps, gaze in the turquoise ball, finger the fragment of red adobe from Pecos, reload the blue Scripto, take a fresh yellow pad, then sit down and see what comes.

Flying nonstop coast to coast, from 21,000 feet at 400 mph, one must look sharp and fast to determine landmarks. Oak Creek, Flagstaff, the sacred peaks of Coconino County, then the ammunition bunkers at Wingate, Gallup an absurdly small civilized scar, and Shiprock visible a hundred miles beyond; then Mt. Taylor, easternmost of the sacred Navajo peaks; and bearing northeast the Jemez range, the Rio Grande, Santa Fe hardly larger than Gallup, the Sangres and the dark blue of Taos Mountain, Eagle Nest and Blue lakes, the red roofs of the Highlands University at Las Vegas; then excitement waning as the Middle West began, checkerboard earth, the three great rivers, Missouri, Mississippi, Ohio, and soon thereafter the sweeping descent to Idylwild. Ocean to ocean in seven hours, breakfast in Malibu, dinner in Manhattan, followed by humid days on the littoral, ameliorated by books and friends, meetings and talk, participated in by the mind earning a living, while the heart went on beating to Mountain Standard Time.

New York, Philadelphia, Pittsburgh, Chicago, Kansas City were heavy stopping stones to Albuquerque, as two planes conked out and four hours were lost. Dinner at last with Erna Fergusson in Old Town as history and folklore, personal reminiscence and kindliness formed the aura of the town's First Lady, now living on a river ranch beneath a cathedral cottonwood.

The next night in Santa Fe I read aloud from Haniel Long's unfinished book and found it good, the ripe work of a writer who waited six decades to write his first novel. This was the fourth visit in two years to Haniel and Alice Long, and again I brought offerings of tea and affection and the feather of a dove; and faintly, very faintly, I envied him his twenty-year head start and his quintessential masterpiece, published in 1936, the *Interlinear to Cabeza de Vaca*.

At dinner on a high point east of town we looked across the river valley to Los Alamos, wickedly winking with lights, while a cottontail nibbled grass outside the window and the flares of sunset reached the zenith.

"You can't do both," Long said. "Lead the administrative life and write."

"I'm trying. And also I want to teach. It's taken me twenty years to learn librarianship. Now I want to teach it."

"I taught for two decades at Carnegie Tech before we came here. I like to think my books continue the process."

"It was your books that brought me here. The wide world's your classroom now."

And to illustrate this, Long gave me a German translation of the *Interlinear*, to add to the French one he gave me a year ago.

Burma born, Harvard schooled, tall, lean, and gray, and suffering the same eye trouble as Huxley's, this man who founded Writer's Editions is humorous, quizzical, wise, and gentle, and I always leave him and his wife with a feeling of refreshment, redetermination, faith, and affection, and the anticipation of the riches which await a man in the decades between fifty and seventy, if he is prepared to recognize them.

"In youth the human body drew me and was the object of my secret and natural dreams. But body after body has taken away from me that sensual phosphorescence which my youth delighted in. Within me is no disturbing interplay now, but only the steady currents of adaptation and of sympathy." Thus speaks Long's conquistador.

The next day I entered the mission church at the Ranchos de Taos, one of the Southwest's two fairest shrines (the other being San Xavier). A party of nuns was being shown through by the priest, and they were having a jolly time, especially the youngest of the lot—a sister whose vitality, unquenched by her funereal habit, led her to peek under the red silk robe of an image to see what was beneath. I had not witnessed such spiritual vigor since Dublin.

Another memorable experience in Taos was the sight of a boy lying in the grass beside a watermelon truck parked by an *acequia*, reading a book, serious, intent, oblivious. When I passed again, hours later, the boy had turned from back to stomach and, propped on his elbow, was writing furiously, purposefully—what?

The sundrenched fields of Taos were lush with alfalfa, goldenrod, and dandelion, exuding midsummer fragrance to the point of asphyxiation. I had been reading *The Man Who Killed the Deer*, and I wanted to see the Blue Lake of the Taoseños. The sign promised a route, but it proved to be only by trail. The road corkscrewed fifteen miles up the Arroyo Hondo, down which white water was foaming. At Twining, elevation 9,412, the road became traversible only by jeep. The air was sharp, and smoke from a campfire rose unwaveringly into an eggshell sky. The bald dome of Mt. Wheeler rose another few thousand feet higher. A trail-sign pointed to Lobo Peak, on whose aspened shoulder I had visited Frieda Lawrence in 1941. An infestation of moths had stripped the aspens, and whole stands of them were shrouded with cocoons, while the filthy worms, known as the Great Basin tent caterpillar, fell in through the car windows.

Two uranium hunters were based here, a Texas father and son, with a Cadillac, a jeep, a scintillator, a forest service map, and a trailerload of grub. Father could have doubled for W. C. Fields. A sign read: "This is private property. You are welcome. Just mind your manners and don't pick the flowers."

The water of the western slope flows to the Rio Grande, and I followed it down the Arroyo Hondo through rocky junipered walls to its confluence with the Great River. The junction of watercourses is a good place to see the river-gods, and I sought to summon them by tossing stones into the bankside mud—the deep primeval ooze which acknowledged my offerings with a pluppity sound of thanks.

After supper I walked on a dirt road in the twilight, through a gate and into a field, with towering trees and Taos Mountain on one side and the Taos plain falling away on the other, clear to the Ranchos and the ranges beyond. I was rapt, remembering that four hundred years of history had passed by here, was quiet, hearing the whisper of ghosts around me, was content to be one link in an endless chain.

Everywhere I went the new edition of the New Mexico State Guide was open on the seat beside me, full of facts and photos and a minimum of misleading information. I never could find the church of San Miguel del Bado as described, or it must have been stuccoed over what the book said was stone, but the side-trip brought an even greater reward.

I had been earlier in Las Vegas, having come over the Sangres from Taos, through the Penitente villages of Picurís and Mora, traversing a high back country of few people and no people, of drizzle and shower and cloud-piled skies, past fields of corn and flowers and heavenly bluebirds, over the haunted route of Coronado, Armijo, and Los Tejanos, of Gregg and Kearny; and in the station there had seen mixed Santa Fe trains, none of which had quickened my pulse—cars, crews, passengers, all ordinary.

And then on this detour, having crossed the Pecos and reached the tiny station of Ribera, I saw a wondrous sight: the westbound Super Chief drawn up on a siding. That meant only one thing: its eastbound counterpart was due, and O Lord! there it was, coming round the turn, the long snake of silver Pullmans drawn by the monstrous red and yellow double diesel, pulling, pulling, with deep-throated, smoking exhausts, horning once for the passing, the engineer riding high on his throne, his gloved hand raised slightly in response to my enthusiastic wave, there at that orgasmic moment of midway meeting; and to crown it all, sight of an old friend, the Pullman car Coconino Princess, on which I had ridden before, coupled between Pine Meadow and Regal Junction, as fair a vision as these eyes have ever seen.

The westbound train gathered speed slowly and I lingered alongside it for several miles, its pony trucks clickety-clicking over the railpoints, until finally it pulled away from me, approaching Glorietta Pass and the descent to Las Vegas and Lamy. All through my lifetime, from the year of my birth, I had ridden over that same rail route, and now I knew that I would never ride that way again, preferring henceforth to go either by air or by auto. The engineer waved as I turned off to Pecos Pueblo, an ancient ruin abandoned in 1838 and now a state monument.

Rain began to fall again, darkening the red soil and the green piñons, and I got soaked while dashing in and out of the ruins of the church, which is dedicated to the same lady as my home town— Nuestra Señora la Reina de los Angeles. Without planning it I found myself traversing Pecos Village and once again following a river to its headwaters, while the car radio transmitted such sentimental songs as to make me long to learn the guitar—songs with apparently no other words than *corazón, amor, alma, y mujer*. Well, what else is there? *Libros*. I had not realized that this fabled river rises in the Sangres, and I preferred the mountain aspect of the stream, lined with a Cistercian monastery and a State Fish Hatchery and the strange modern hacienda of Arnold B. Friedman, to the lower Pecos country of Billy the Kid and worse.

This search for the source is a philosophical urge, as well as physiographical, a blind going upward to the beginning of things, while the world narrows in and all else is eliminated. This focus on the basic elements is purifying, therapeutic, electrifying, and this way of re-charging by stripping away is a dedicatory one, well suited to this Angeleno who lives ordinarily in the midst of multiplicity. Such were my thoughts up where the Pecos rises.

The day's showers had been only a prelude to the storm I saw gath-ering overhead, and so I reluctantly wheeled around at the first pos-sible point. It was the yard of a Justice of the Peace, who had thought-fully provided his front porch with a bed, though sans mattress. A long way from the neoned wedding chapels of the Lower Sonoran. The cloudburst came as I regained Pecos Village, and the world dis-appeared behind a curtain of water, then just as quickly the clouds broke and the blueness of the sky made the eyes ache.

Sum it up. The spirit of religion, the sense of layered history, the enormous beauty of landscape under the blue and white sky and the starry darkness, a land of many-cultured richness lived in for at least a millenium and yet still sparsely peopled—these are some of the essences that northern New Mexico holds for me and which I find nowhere else on earth. Land of enchantment, land of nourishment, land of many good returns.

East of the Sandias the road runs north to Golden and Madrid. What's in a name? Much—especially if the name is foreign and musical. When asked for the most musical words in English, regardless of meaning, a foreigner replied "cellar door." Thus the Sandias, to one ignorant of Spanish. The Watermelon Mountains? Well, yes, as long as the mind doesn't visualize the seedy fruit.

The Sandia Mountains. How different they appear when seen from the east, dark green and wooded all the way up, humped like a whale, without the bare face they present to Albuquerqueans. Southernmost of their sacred peaks, the range was called Turtle Mountain by the Pueblos. The turnoff to the crest was alluring, but I had miles to go before I parked, and the compass pointed north. Golden? Hardly.

Madrid? A company coal town, obviously misnamed. The beauty of this lonely route lay in the piñon forest, and in the clouds that were beginning to cap the sky.

For it was another summer, and the daily thundershowers had begun. I was free of desk and phone and daily mail, and the people to whom must be given, if one wishes to get. I had gained New Mexico again with empty reservoirs, a week's prospect of pure isolation from the usual and a return home brimful of beauty.

At Cerrillos I came to an unexpected crossing of the railroad, the main line of the Santa Fe, and on a hunch I turned off and cruised through the village. I stopped by a group of natives on the porch of the grocery. "Any trains due?" I asked, briskly. Whereupon one of them lurched toward me, preceded by his boozy breath. "My friend," he pronounced, "there passes here one train every half hour," and he staggered back to his fellows. They laughed, as I drove on, crossed the tracks, and reconnoitered. Not a sound or sign of life, only shining rails. Then I spied a lank sack hanging from the trackside hook, and a car parked alongside, with a woman sleeping in it. The mail train was due. I waited, and pretty soon heard the low hum of an approaching diesel. A full five minutes passed before it burst round the curve, heading northeast to Lamy and Las Vegas, and bore down on the station with overriding urgency. The Super Chief, no less. The sack was hooked in, and an equally thin one thrown off. The silver vision passed. Toroweap, Tierra Amarilla, Cloudcroft, but this time my Princess was coupled elsewhere. The woman got out, picked up the sack, drove off. I had witnessed the postmistress of Cerrillos at work.

I paid my first visit to the Museum on the outskirts of Santa Fe, and saw an exhibition of contemporary arts and crafts of great beauty; silver and wood, turquoise and wool, the elements worked by hand with loving skill, the objects displayed in imaginative ways, to give one of the best museum experiences I have ever had.

City of the Holy Faith, huddle of abodes, cottonwooded, piñoned,

ringed by ranges with ringing names: the Sangre de Cristos, the Sandias, the Jemez. Day's end and the mountains were blue black; again
a lone rabbit, this time a big-eared jack, nibbling and sniffing his way
across the somnolent landscape, as I looked north to the last light on
Truchas, knowing that the morrow would find me on upland slopes.

The morrow was Sunday, and I saw people in their best, as once
again I left the highway and took a dirt road to Chimayó and beyond,
a gentle climb against the flow of water, past fields and flowers and
burdened orchards. "Cherries, cherries," cried the children, from
where they crouched by the roadside, holding out handfuls of the
little red fruit.

All the beautiful choices were mine, whether to seek the fabled
santos in the Santuario of Chimayó or, to see the Valley of Cordova,
where Joseph Krumgold made *And Now Miguel*, that almost unbear-
ably beautiful documentary film of sheepherding and a small boy's
dream. One must always choose among several, and Truchas was my
choice, an ancient village lying exposed on a hogback, inanimate on
this Sunday morning, yet eternally alive, as the ghost towns of Arizona are not. Metals were not the reason for Truchas' naked site. The
villagers built there originally for defense against their enemies, descending to the fields, or driving their sheep to mountain meadows.

I stopped and read in the guidebook: "In March 1772 an archive
records the request of the villagers for twelve muskets and powder
and protection from the Comanche. (Request denied). The walls of
the adobe houses here are unusually thick (Truchas is a very cold place
in winter). On a clear day are visible the La Plata Mountains 150 miles
away in Southern Colorado; and Mt. Taylor, 150 miles south of west.''

It was not *quite* that clear.

I crawled along the spinal street, seeing a crocheted peacock in a
window, potted geraniums everywhere, a rainbow painted wall and
matching eaves (someone was crazy for color), stacked woodpiles,
and I breathed piñon smoke from cooking stoves.

At the general store I threaded a knot of black-garbed elders (no drunkenness here, but serious talk, of *agua* and *mujeres* and *caballos*, my ears told me) and browsed the merchandise, while drinking a 7-Up. Denim, gingham, leather, and straw were some of the staples my fingers felt, as I inhaled the dry-goods smell common to J. W. Robinson, Selfridge's, La Belle Jardinière, or wherever on earth.

Once again choice was necessary, and I bore north over piney slopes instead of climbing higher toward the Truchas Peaks and the next highest point in New Mexico (Wheeler Peak, 13,151 feet; North Truchas Peak, 13,110 feet). I came at last to the *cor cordium* of Spanish New Mexico, the ancient village of Las Trampas. It was noon and the priest had locked the church and gone to lunch. So had everyone. The pueblo-like plaza was deserted, except for a car with Montana plates, but I could feel eyes on me, as I prowled around the classic church of Santo Tomás del Rio de las Trampas, coming on a store of wooden crosses piled against the rear wall, evidence that this was indeed deep penitente country. At the front corner hung the only remaining bell, named *Gracia* because of its gentle tone—and this I verified with steady strokes of my strongest finger.

Leaving the village and descending toward Peñasco on the Rio Pueblo, I met a rodeo of pickup trucks and young men in white shirts and a short distance beyond I saw a girl in a red dress disappearing through the piñons.

Entering Taos I got another sense of eternals from sight of my old watermelon truck, parked in the same place alongside the *acequia*, but honestly I cannot say the boy was reading. He must have finished the book and taken up something else.

And here, too, was the ubiquitous smell of burning piñon, recalling Peattie's words in his book on trees: "They say that those who, like Kit Carson, had once known the bells, the women and the pinyon smoke of Taos could never stay away—come Kiowa, come Sioux, come Kansas blizzard or calabozo."

El Crepusculo carried news of the death in San Diego of Bert Phillips, one of Taos' founding artists, and of the visit of Frieda Lawrence's

daughter Barbara while Frieda's husband Angie was in Italy. I found
Frieda in the house on the plain at El Prado, thanks to the directions
of Joe Montoya's son at the family service station, where he was being aided by a swarm of boys, each of whom performed one auto-
motive chore in slow motion, a pleasant change from metropolitan
"minute men" service. I had not seen Frieda in five years, and found
her still a fountain of friendly vitality. If Swift and Pope and the other
bachelor misanthropes could have known a woman like Frieda, English literature would have been different, in the way it differed through
what she gave Lawrence; and as we sat over tea and biscuits and spun
the thread of talk clear back to the fateful day she first saw him in
flannels and blazer and red beard, launching cockshell boats for her
children, I knew that this was basic to all literary history, that literature is made by men *and* women, a fact best understood by French
critics.

South of Eagle Nest, State Highway 38 takes off to the east, giving
promise, on the map, of a graded road over the mountains to Mora.
The promise was not kept. What appeared on paper to be a beautiful
back road was actually a deteriorating set of ruts, suited only to truck
or jeep. I was driving a Chevrolet coupé, albeit a powerful eight-
cylinder job, and with the automatic transmission which, contrary to
popular belief, is excellent for slow driving over wretched roads,
because of the uniform flow of power that can be maintained down to
standstill and start again. And the car was high-bedded enough to
clear the boulders; so it went, but just.

The road began alluringly enough along the adobe edges of sloping
meadows. Still I had an eye on the sky. It was beginning to pile up
with clouds that would break with rain before the day was ended,
and I didn't want to be on 'dobe when they did.

There was no sign of life, even at the occasional ranches. The highway markers were rusted and illegible, and there was an increasing
number of *trancas*, gated fences, requiring all my strength to manip-

ulate. My eyes lifted to the blue mesa toward which the road climbed. Black Lake lay to the right, a natural *ciénaga* edged with deep grass and herds of fattening Herefords. This was the last place to turn back, but I did not know it, and pressed on ignorantly past the point of no return.

Suddenly the road narrowed and grew rockier. I drove at five miles an hour, grunting and sweating, in shorts and sneakers, thankful that my arms were stronger than my foresight, and really very happy not to be on Wilshire Boulevard. My comfort was a fresh set of tire tracks; otherwise I would not have known which choice to make when the road forked, as it did again and again.

Gaining the mesa at last I paused and looked back to the northern-most Sangres in the distance—Wheeler, Pueblo, and Lobos peaks, those bare "cloud-capp'd towers"—wondering how long I had be-fore the rain came, and if there were *caliche* ahead, then turned my back on 'em and resumed my forward motion. The "road" rutted rockily through ponderosas and Engelmanns, then turned into a boul-dered trough, down which I caromed toward what the map called Coyote Creek. It seemed to flow into the Guadalupita Valley, even-tually to Mora and what, by contrast, would be civilization. This was the very opposite of the experience of seeking the headwaters of the Pecos and the Hondo: I longed to leave the headwaters, my muscles rigid under the hot flow of sweat, compelled to control my desire to hurry and beat the rain, and instead to crawl, bump, bounce, creep, and slither, holding horsepower and heartbeat in check. It had rained the day before, and the road was pooled and treacherous. And the flowers that bloom in the summer tra la got only sidelong looks from this scion of an old horticultural family. *¡Qué lástima!*

Then the trough tossed me into a clearing—a sawmill, with prom-ise of human beings, of whom I had not seen one since Eagle Nest three hours before. It was a big establishment, with many sheds and cabins and parked trucks, and piles of trimmings. But no saw buzzed. No voice spoke. There was no stock-pile of logs.

Nada. Nadi Ninguno. En ninguna parte. The quintessence of nothingness. God, but it was eerie, like something out of Poe or Melville. I whistled. Echo answered. The tracks ended at still another fenced gate, leading to a ford over the creek. I parked and went around and faced a sign, and read, ABSOLUTELY NO TRESPASSING. Too late. I had already trespassed. Was this Highway 38, a public thoroughfare of the sovereign state of New Mexico, or was it a private road of the woodcutters? Had I taken a wrong turn up on the mesa?

And then I smelled and saw smoke, coming from a cabin chimney at the far end of the clearing. I trudged over spongy sawdust earth and called *¡Hola!* Two heads popped out of two windows, like boxed jacks, one red, one black. Grown boys, they belonged to, their mouths full of food, their eyes of astonishment.

"Where am I?" I asked. "Can I get out?"

They laughed and came outdoors. El Rojo was an Anglo, El Moro an *hijo de pais* who had stumps for hands.

"This is the sawmill of the Ortega Brothers," said Red, and Blackie added, "Where you from?"

"From Eagle Nest, Black Lake, and down the road to hell," I replied.

Again they laughed. "The worst is over," they assured me.

"Through the gate to Mora?"

"Sure, but don't be in a hurry. Those rocks are hungry."

"Where is everyone?" I asked.

"Logging. We just brought in a load and stopped for lunch."

"I have sweat the hunger out of me," I said.

"Where do you live?" they asked.

"In the City of Angels," I replied, "and I bring you blessings from Nuestra Señora."

They crossed themselves automatically, thinking perhaps I was a priest, garbed for a swim, and as I went back to my car, I heard them banging around in their cabin, whooping like Indians.

"The worst is over" was a way of speaking. The "road" forded and reforded Coyote Creek (a lovely stream under other conditions), shelving high along the bank on one side and then the other, rain-pooled, rocky, ribbon-narrow, dropping me fast with thunder at my back, and the only good omen a flight of blue birds across the very hood of the car.

The canyon kept widening, however, and the flow of sweat had slackened, my muscles relaxed, and I came at last to an angel—a wo-man in a white dress who vanished into her cabin as I drove up. In the window was the face of her daughter, who spoke sweetly in the grave manner of the country, when I asked her where I was.

"Guadalupita Valley," she said. "You bring rain with you. Gracias, señor."

"The road is better?"

"Truly a fine road hereafter."

"Thank you, thank you!" I said, as if she were personally respon-sible for this engineering miracle.

Shortly thereafter I turned off the road for a drive of cattle, headed for the high summer pastures, and I marveled at the working horses and their riders, Anglos all, with unfriendly eyes.

The rain caught up with me as I reached Guadalupita store and stopped to drink a cold bottle of soda pop, utterly relaxed as the fall turned to hail, then back to rain and finally to drip, cool on my hot skin. I snapped on the car radio and it crackled hopelessly with static.

At village edge I picked up a one-legged man, who raised a stick to stop me, and took him along my way to Mora. His name was Jesús Dorado, aged sixty-seven, bachelor, native of the valley, grower of pinto beans. Almost toothless, unshaven, dirty-overalled and smelly, Señor Dorado was essentially a gentleman, affable, informed as to the history and topography of the region, almost urbane, a representative spokesman for the land in his time. And he was amazed that I had come over that wild road in a city car.

The valley continued to widen as we neared Mora. West north-west the triple peaks of Truchas formed the horizon. Beyond the eastern hills lay plains and rivers, the Ozarks, the Appalachians—pallid country, all of it. My compass swung west southwest.

I had not liked Mora on my first visit, and I liked it even less this time, sensing there a focus of evil forces, personified by a horseman leading another horse, an Anglo of such debauched visage as to chill my blood.

Rolling down the road to Vegas I had an exciting glimpse of an all but naked girl in a roadside *acequia*, and I thought of Frank Waters' *People of the Valley*, laid in this very region, with its beautiful episode of Maria and the soldier at the pool; and I was uncertain as to which is the more memorable and lasting, literature or life.

Another day I lunched with Waters at Los Alamos, where he too serves the University of California, as information officer, and I sensed no dichotomy between the man and his work, as is the case in writers of lesser craft and character.

Flying back to Albuquerque in a Carco Beechcraft, I experienced a feeling of flight not possible in a large plane. We blew off The Hill's landing strip like a leaf in the wind, and floated out over the valley of the Rio Grande, as the mesa fell away steeply beneath us. I sat alongside the pilot, three other passengers in the seat behind us, and he pointed out the pueblos as we passed over them, following the serpentine source of life, matrix of New Mexican history and culture, fed by snow and spring, the grand configuration now visible in a glance, comprehensible in its symbiotic parts, once seen all snowy frozen on a flight in winter, then as a golden belt of cottonwoods in November, and now green green, summer green, on this last river flight, under an immensity of clouds which left shadows on the earth.

Rain and the Beechcraft fell together on the airport at Albuquerque, and I stood around on the edge of the cool curtain while waiting for a westbound plane. Belted down in TWA's Flight 82, then circling north over the city, I had a last sight of the Sandias and a final good omen, not one but two perfect rainbows—*circo iris*, *arcobaleno*, *arc-en-ciel*, *regenbogen*, *rainbow*, take your choice, all beautiful, all blessed—arching from Bernalillo to where Highway 66 breached the range.

It was a turbulent flight, too rough to serve food and drink, and I buckled down and read the society page of the *Santa Fe New Mexican*, able to absorb only the frothiest of prose.

Phoenix was hot, windy, sandy. I stayed belted in the plane.

Approaching the Colorado, we overtook the high brown front of the sandstorm, and then saw the river at Blythe, looped like silver on the dark body of earth, while the western sky gave the day angry ending, symbolic of the struggle between the states for the Southwest's most precious element. The land beneath me was California.

The Way It Sounds to Me

I WRITE about the way it sounds to me. Not the way it is. No. The way it sounds. Music, I mean. I write not to instruct, but to entertain, and, I hope, delight, the way music delights, by a mingling of sound and sense. For I am not merely a librarian, but am something worse, something better — a musical failure. I wanted more than anything else to be a composer, but I had no talent for composition. I was a good performer in my youth. Before marijuana was even heard of, I got the same effects, and merely from music itself. I was musically well brought up, by a piano teacher, a woman, who weighed 250 pounds. I was physically afraid of her, for she made me practice, and once she picked me off the stool like a puppy and shook me, then slammed me down and snarled—''Now will you play it the way it reads?'' I was always sneaking in bits of my own, corrupting the text, perverting the dynamics — a precocious little Stokowski.

Years passed, and by the time I reached my twenties I recognized the truth, that I was not and never would be a composer. So I burned my woodwinds, dynamited my piano, and left music for language. More years have passed, and I have persisted in learning how to write, to be a writer. Always though with music in my mind, in my blood; and, I hope, in my words.

I write about two things: playing music and hearing music. Fortunate is he who can do both. Man has a need to participate. He is not meant to stand alone. Making music together with other men and women is one of the most satisfying things a man can do. We have all seen how music transforms those who are making it.

I was up in Montana once, to speak at the dedication of a new library, and the ceremonies opened with the inevitable singing by the high school glee club. I've seen a lot of homely kids, but when that group of country boys and girls filed in and lined up, wearing the inevitable robes, I thought, this is a new low in homely awkwardness. Then they began to sing—and before my eyes I saw them transformed by the alchemy of music from ugly brats to radiant angels, rapt and transfigured. And I thought of a poem, as I often do in moments of strong emotion, a poem by Siegfried Sassoon called "Everyone Sang":

> *Everyone suddenly burst out singing:*
> *And I was filled with such delight*
> *As prisoned birds must find in freedom*
> *Winging wildly across the white*
> *Orchards and dark green fields; on, on, and out of sight.*
> *Everyone's voice was suddenly lifted*
> *And beauty came like the setting sun.*
> *My heart was shaken with tears, and horror*
> *Drifted away . . . O, but everyone*
> *Was a bird; and the song was wordless;*
> *The singing will never be done.*

Once upon a time I was a student in France. It was not long after I had abandoned music for literature, and I had occasional moments of weakness and doubt. I missed playing ensemble. I was lonely. And then I had a wonderful experience.

One day I was walking down the Rue de la Liberté in Dijon, the old ducal capital of Burgundy. Though the main street, it is narrow and crooked, and often the sidewalk shrinks and dumps one into the street. I was passing the town's music store, and I heard a violin being played. It was *what* was being played that transfixed me—the opening phrases of César Franck's Violin Sonata. Has any other sonata an opening to match it—tender and grave, at once questioning and assertive, a restrained dialogue between violin and piano, asking, telling, leading slowly to marriage and union, all sounds resolved in mutual fulfillment?

I stood there in front of the shop, while the sidewalk crowd flowed around me, and listened to the violin. Someone was just fiddling around, as the saying goes; trying out an instrument, perhaps; starting, stopping, tuning — but always the same phrases, always the César Franck, and without the answering piano.

It was a sibylline summons to me, for only the year before I had played the piano part of the Franck sonata in a student recital. I entered the store. The music was coming from the rear. It was a young woman playing. Though her back was turned to me, I recognized her as the violinist in a string ensemble that played gypsy music in the town's leading café. I sat down at a piano and played the first notes of the sonata, softly, timidly, questioningly. She turned around, her eyes flashing. I stopped. "No!" she cried. "Don't stop! Play!"

I did. She did. We did. It was ragged in places, but we never ceased until we had played it through; and when we had finished, an audience had gathered. It was France, a provincial town, a beautiful town where people have more time for spontaneous things. And when we had finished, altogether hot and sweaty and happy, the proprietor closed the store early and set everyone up for chilled *vin blanc* in the nearest café.

Once in San Diego I heard music that sounded good to me coming when it did, and that evoked memories of my years of music-making. I had flown in from the east. We had crossed the Colorado at Yuma, and in the late afternoon light the river was meandering and relaxed, its long course nearly ended, the waters of its final tributary, the Gila, gathered in its flow. Unlike my illustrious namesake, who first descended the Colorado in a boat, I have made only aerial surveys of the river. It is a beautiful watercourse from the air, accepting tributaries in junction after junction; the Gunnison, the Green, the San

Juan, the Virgin, the Little Colorado—confluent waters, heavy with silt until they drop their burden in Lake Mead, then spin the turbines at Hoover Dam to bring the electric power that has ruined Los Angeles' climate; and finally make their crystalline getaway to the Gulf, dividing Arizona and California in more ways than one.

In San Diego I registered at the U. S. Grant Hotel, relished a cold sea-food dinner, then went for a walk. A Marine band was tuning up on the Broadway bandstand—a band of eager beavers ready to blow every last kink out of horn, trumpet, and woodwind. I didn't think I could take it, and so I returned to the hotel, undressed, and stretched out peacefully on the bed. I was still hearing the music of Bach that had been playing earlier—the Goldberg Variations, with the theme which says *found*, *loved*, *lost*, or in greater terms of life, *born*, *lived*, *died*; and the best of all music was still pulsing in my veins with soundless eloquence.

Then the band began to play, with such violence and volume as to be heard all the way back to Pima County. I got up and uselessly closed the window. The music was coming through the walls. And gradually it seduced me. The way those kids were playing Sousa, even a cigar-store Indian would have begun to beat time and to march. Perhaps they were just home from Korea or just leaving for there; in any case, they were playing with all their hearts and other organs. I got up and opened the window and began to march around the room, ready for anything, to go anywhere, which is of course what the composer intended.

And then the music changed, as they played a band arrangement of music from *Porgy and Bess*, best of all American music since MacDowell. Again I collapsed on the bed, completely undone; and when a single trumpet played "Bess, Yo' Is My Woman Now," the way it sounded to me was heavenly. It took me back twenty-five years to the last time I had heard music in San Diego—trumpet music, too: Bach, up on the boat-deck of a ship in the harbor. It was the *S. S. Yale*, coastwise steamer between San Diego, San Pedro, and San Francisco, and I was the saxophone player in the ship's orchestra.

It was the summer of 1928. After school was out, I had been per-suaded by well-meaning, obnoxious friends to give up music and get a so-called healthful outdoor job that would build me up from a busy year of classes by day and dance music and worse by night. I have never believed in exercise, and after two weeks of wheeling cement on the college campus I was ready for a breakdown. Those enormous barrows of sloppy stuff weighed more than I did, and every time I poured one into the conduit ditch, I nearly went in with it.

The only thing that made the job endurable was the friend I was working with. During our lunch hour and in the short evening before we turned in early, we read aloud Meredith's "Modern Love," and also the poetry of Rossetti, Hardy, and Robinson Jeffers. And we drank a lot—milk.

One day I returned to the fraternity house after work and found a telegram from San Diego. It was from a musician I had once played with—a pianist who directed the orchestra on the *Yale*—offering me the tenor saxophone job, starting the next morning when the ship called at San Pedro en route north.

"You're not going to take it, are you?" my friend asked.

I hit him as hard as I could, and ducked, for he was twice my size—an ideal type for wheeling cement. Then I rushed to my room and made sure my reeds were good ones. I always used Vandoren reeds, and an ebony mouthpiece inlaid with silver.

I was dockside in San Pedro the next morning when the *Yale* ar-rived—a slim white vessel with thin black stacks. Lord how she pitched and rolled, when she rounded Point Concepcion and met those northwest swells in from Alaska!

The first morning was spent in rehearsing. The piano player was a little tyrant and a first-class musician, and we played everything from his manuscript arrangements. He was like my old piano teacher—a classicist, intolerant of improvisation—and his bible was Bach. He was one of the earliest jazz musicians to discover the gold mine in the *Well-Tempered Clavichord*. His arrangements were full of ingenuity and high spirits—good music for the time and the place.

The *Yale* was at sea four nights a week, in harbor three; and in the wrong harbor—San Diego. Our sister ship, the *Harvard*, was the lucky one, berthed three nights in San Francisco. The *Yale* docked in San Francisco at ten in the morning, and sailed south again mid-afternoon of the same day, not allowing much time to do the things youth likes to do, yet we managed to do them anyway.

What about the trumpet music of Bach that I thought of when I heard the Marine bandsmen playing Gershwin? Our pianist on the *Yale* doubled in brass. He could play the piano with his left hand, the trumpet with his right, and the crowd loved it. Off duty he would sit hunched up in his bunk and play a Bach partita for unaccompanied instrument until he made you cry; or he would set off the pyrotechnics of a Bach fugue until you saw the rockets burst.

We had returned to ship one night from our broadcast over a local radio station, just as the bugler on one of the Navy ships in harbor was playing Taps.

"I'll show that s– of a b– how to play Taps!" cried our little hero in a frenzy, as he unpacked his trumpet and rushed up to the boat deck of the *Yale*. He was high in every sense. We had made one stop, between the station and the ship, and our whistles were still wet, especially his.

Then came the fieriest exhibition of virtuosity I have ever heard. He not only played Taps and variations on it, but also every other bugle call in the armed forces of all the nations, and then Bach, until the entire inner harbor of San Diego, thronged with anchored vessels, was ringing with music.

Then signal lights began to wink from ship to ship, as commanding officers grew confused. What was happening? Was it war or peace, Taps or Reveille?

A Navy launch came alongside and we were hailed. "Who's doing that?" was the cry. "An enlisted man?"

"Hell no!" was the answer. "It's Gabriel!"

In these my middle years, at once more stormy and more peaceful than those of my youth, I have come to love the poetry of Yeats, and I find myself reading again and again the letter he wrote in his early seventies to his younger friend Dorothy Wellesley. It was after he had been ill and was convalescent that he wrote to her, "Part of my sense of solitude was that I felt I would never know that supreme experience of life—that I think possible to the young—to share profound thought and then to touch."

Is there anything as thrilling as to hear great music—share profound thought—with a beloved? Yes, of course, or nearly so. To hear it alone. Sometimes I escape from campus on a Friday afternoon and go by myself to the Philharmonic concert. Once a cellist was to play the Dvořák Concerto—music almost too rich for my blood— and was seated restlessly on stage, with instrument between his knees and bow in hand, waiting through the orchestral opening for his entrance, when he saw a small piece of white paper on the platform in front of him. It bothered him, and he reached toward it as if his bow were a stick with a nail in its end, and tried to spear the paper.

The audience tittered, and the conductor turned around and felt to see if his clothes were in order. The audience laughed. The cellist pointed at the piece of white paper. The conductor looked puzzled, then grinned. The orchestra kept playing, of course, and finally the soloist reached out his bow and scraped the paper along the floor to where he could bend over, pick it up, and pocket it, barely in time to make his somber entry in the solo part.

Music is all around us; above, below, in and out, almost as universal and beautiful as Love itself, from which all music comes; and one hears it wherever he goes. Take the music of the penny-whistle I once heard in the streets of Chartres. I had gone alone to see the cathedral for the first time; and all morning I had drifted in and out and around the gemlike building whose beauty is beyond my power to describe. Then I ate lunch in a workers' restaurant and was having a *café* on the sidewalk, when I heard the music approach.

A street air, it was, played on a penny-whistle, at regular intervals; monotonous and haunting. As it came nearer, I saw its maker: a middle-aged peasant, lean and brown and with grape leaves in his leather hat, wearing leather pants and jacket. A peddler—probably a Basque —of goat cheeses carried in a wicker basket on his back. In his hand was a wooden whistle, a pipe with stops, and every few moments he put it to his lips and played his tune, which meant of course, "Buy my cheeses, come buy my cheeses."

And I did, hypnotized by the music to do his will. Somehow I managed to accost him and buy a cheese—God knows why, for I don't like cheese, goat cheese least of all. And I saw his face, his yellow-brown-green eyes—but he never saw me. He looked through and beyond me, his mind on distant things. And this is remarkable: his breath smelled fresh, like a cow's. That man had been eating grass. Man? The Great God Pan.

The final episode in this suite of musical tales is about the most unmusical of all music—the sounds made by the bagpipe. The hero is a Scot, of course. He was a big man, built like a bulldozer, and silenter. Throughout the ten-day voyage on a freighter from London to New York, he paid no attention to the rest of the passengers. There were only half a dozen of us, including my wife and me; an English nurse from Nyasaland; an older Englishwoman from Bedford—an exuberant woman who had borne twelve children and was en route to visit one of them in what she was certain was the Indian-infested wilderness of Iowa; an extroverted American theatrical agent, caged like a tiger on the recreation-free freighter; and finally the dour Scot, whose name was John Douglas.

He was not rude. He said the necessary minimum of social phrases but no more. I thought at first he was just big and dumb and bored, with no inner life and not much of an outer one, and I christened him somewhat contemptuously "Johnny Scot." Midway across the Atlantic I witnessed something which was a clue to the real man, but it was I who was too dumb at the time to know it.

I had arisen at daybreak and started up from the boat deck, where the few passenger cabins were, to the hurricane deck above the bridge.

As I mounted the ladder and peered over the top, I saw Johnny Scot with his back to me. I stopped and stared, for he was dancing, a solo Highland Fling, that intricate one in and out of imaginary crossed swords, and with such delicacy of movement as to make his two hundred pounds seem featherweight. He was dancing to music of his own making, whistling a bagpipe tune—a two-part tune, with droning bass and squealing treble. I watched, and listened, in awe, unbeknownst for a long minute, before I backed silently down the ladder.

Then it came to be the last night before New York. We were about fifty miles off coast, a moonless June night, the Milky Way banding heaven clear across, from Scorpio in the south to Stella Polaris in the north. We were running through a fleet of becalmed sailing boats—little ones, "R" boats, perhaps, like tired butterflies—in regatta from Providence to Newport. They had the right-of-way, and our freighter, its outspoken captain from Flatbush on the bridge, was having artfully to steer among them.

All of us passengers were up on the hurricane deck—even Johnny Scot—and the theatrical agent, seeing everyone peaceful, had to stir things up, by proposing that we play that old parlor game of going round the circle and each telling the story of the most moving incident in his or her life.

Johnny's turn came last. I thought he would pass, with the Scottish equivalent of "no comment." I was wrong. I was never more wrong. He told a story, a most wonderful story, in an expressionless voice, with an accent thick as the porridge in his native land.

"I was an officer with His Majesty's Forces," he said, "and after the war I was in Vienna, in charge of military police, in the British zone. We had many civilian employees, from several countries. One was an Italian girl from a hill-town named Terradoro. Her name was Giulia. She was young and beautiful, with long dark hair and large dark eyes. She was small too. Came hardly to my shoulder. I called her my Italian friend.

"Time came for her to return to Italy and on the last day in the office she came to me and said she wanted a souvenir. 'What do you

want?' I asked. She opened a drawer in my desk. It was full of con-
fiscated firearms. She picked out a small gold-handled revolver—a
beautiful little killer—and said she wanted it.

"I told her no. It was against all the rules. The weapons were in-
ventoried, and besides, it meant the death penalty for any civilian
caught with arms of any kind.

"She kept begging for the gun, and I finally gave in. First though I
did two things. I removed the cartridge chamber and kept it, and
then I made her take a vow never to reveal to anyone under any cir-
cumstances where she had obtained the gun. Then she returned to
Italy."

He paused and lit a cigarette, and in the matchflare I saw his rugged
face, wearing no expression. We were quiet, waiting for him to
resume.

"Six months passed," he said at last. "And I got a long furlough. I
had never been to Italy and I had a strong desire to see Giulia again.
She had stopped writing. So I took a jeep and went over the Brenner
Pass. Nice scenery too, those Alps—if I hadn't seen the Highlands
first.

"I arrived at the village, near Florence, toward evening, parked
the jeep, and entered the local tavern. When I asked for her, the
place fell silent. Perhaps it was my accent. I had learned only bits of
Italian from her—those few necessary words a man learns from a
woman—but they knew who it was I wanted.

"After a few rounds of wine, on me, I persuaded the tavern-keep-
er's wife to talk. I learned that Giulia was in prison. For life. The
charge? Illegal possession of firearms. She had shown her souvenir to
a supposed friend and had been denounced to the American soldiery
as a Communist agent.

"They told me that she had been offered her freedom if she would
tell who gave her the revolver. She wouldn't tell. They even tor-
tured her. Still she wouldn't talk. She never talked.

"And so because the revolver was incapable of being fired, she got a life sentence, instead of the death penalty which would otherwise have been hers.''

Again he stopped and smoked in silence. It was probably the most talking he had done in a long while, and he was out of breath. Then he spoke again.

''I went to the American military headquarters early next morning, and because I was a high-ranking officer, I got through to the Colonel in charge. I told him where Giulia had obtained the gun. The Colonel sent for the transcript of the trial. It was brief. He read it through, then wrote out a summary order for her release.''

The Scot looked at me then and said, ''You Americans can get things done in a hurry when you want to.'' I warmed to the compliment, then cooled when he added, ''Most of the time they're the wrong things.''

''I took the order for her release,'' he continued, ''and drove to the women's prison in the outskirts of Florence. It was still early, and when they led me to the ward where Giulia was confined, I saw her through the bars, sitting with her back to me, combing her hair. Ah but the lass had beautiful hair.''

At that point I thought I detected a rising half-degree of warmth in his voice, but I couldn't be sure. It might have been merely his accent.

''Then she put on her stockings,'' he said. ''Still with her back to me. I waited for her to hold them up and look for runs, the way women do, before I called her name.

''She jumped up as if she had been shot in the back and turned around, and her face was terrible to see—terrible and wonderful and beautiful, all at once.

'' 'Oh Johnny!' she said, and sat down again. 'You've come to visit me. How good of you.'

'' 'No, lass,' I said, 'I've come to take you out.' And the warden, who'd come with me, held up the Colonel's order and nodded yes.

''She got up again then, and came toward the door like a sleepwalker, and at that moment the turnkey opened the door, and she walked on through, and she put her arm through my arm and her cheek against my cheek—and 'Oh Johnny' was all she could say, over and over and over.''

He stopped then, and it was a long while before anything was said. Then the woman from Bedford asked, in that matter-of-fact way the English have, ''Then what happened, Mr. Douglas?''

I thought the Scot never would rouse himself and answer, but at last he did, almost inaudibly.

''Then what happened? Not very much. I had never seen Venice, and so I put her in the jeep, and we drove as far as we could, and then I hired a gondola, and we went all the way.''

With that he got up and descended the ladder to the cabin deck, and we heard his door close. It was the next morning when I saw him again, and again he was his old solitary silent self. We were off Ambrose Lightship for the pilot, then approaching the most beautiful landfall in the world for a homesick American, all of us at the landward rail—all but Johnny Scot; he was at the rail, yes, at the seaward rail, the rail that looked back to the Old World.

By midafternoon we had cleared quarantine and were docked on the Hudson side of Manhattan, along about Twenty-sixth Street. The Scot didn't more than nod goodbye to any of us, and the last I ever saw of him he was walking off the pier alone, making his sure and delicate way like a dancer among the obstacles of freight and baggage, carrying his worldly goods in the form of two large duffle bags. And he was whistling, that darned bagpipe tune.

The Double Marriage of Robinson Jeffers

I SHALL approach my subject in a conservative way, as befits a middle-aged librarian, by quoting from a book which, if it is not *the* good book, is at least *a* very good book. Webster, I mean. Ours is an age of facts and statistics, of the isolation of ascertainable data. Emotion is suspect, feeling taboo. I have strong feelings about my subject, yet I also have facts to support them which I began compiling at Occidental College, thirty years ago, as a student of those inspiring teachers of English, C. F. McIntyre and B. F. Stelter. In asking the reader to share my feelings about Robinson Jeffers' poetry, I shall use some of these facts to build a footing for us as we go—a few granite steppingstones for our feet, while our minds are carried far and wide by this poet's lofty lines.

What does Webster have to say about poets?

A poet is one who makes, invents, or composes original fables, fictions and the like. One endowed with great imaginative, emotional, or intuitive power and capable of expressing his conceptions, passions or intuitions in language marked by poetic beauty.

My approach then is two-pronged, since in addition to asking what Jeffers has made, I intend to inquire also into what has made him, to seek the major determinants in his gradual transformation from the teen-age graduate of half a century ago, enamored of sports and mountain climbing, to one of the great poets of our time who, by his devoted labor, has slowly come to occupy one of the few niches literature reserves for major poets.

A great poet does not just happen, nor can he be made to order. He is the result of powerful forces operating on a strong and a sensitive organism. Education, parentage, environment, for example; a woman, a war, economic want or security.

We are ignorant of what made Homer and Shakespeare great, for we do not know who these mysterious men were—the two greatest poets the world has ever produced—but we do know what exile did to Dante; or the effect of Italy on Browning; of the Irish revolution on Yeats; and of the Civil War on Walt Whitman. Change and growth are hallmarks of great poetry. Think of the progress from *Venus and Adonis* to *King Lear* and its supreme line "Ripeness is all"; or from "I sing the body electric" to "When lilacs last in the dooryard bloom'd"; and from "I will arise and go now, and go to Innisfree" to "Under bare Ben Bulben's head/In Drumcliff Churchyard Yeats is laid."

Lesser poets do not change and grow, for change and growth are agonies, almost unbearable, and for a poet to be true to his genius, and write what "the tall angel" says he must write, means that he must avoid the soft sand of easy success and walk where the sharp rocks are hard and the footing firm.

To illustrate the change and growth that Robinson Jeffers experienced, I shall cite two of his short poems published only a dozen years apart. The first dates from 1912, and is called "On the Cliff"; it is about the Palos Verdes in Southern California:

> *Do you remember, dear, that little house*
> *Built high against the high cliff's ragged brows*
> *Over the emerald ocean's level floor*
> *Where we were sitting, while the quick day wore*
> *To sunset? Ah, how swiftly the day passed,*
> *Our day, our one sweet day that would not last.*
> *Altho' we did not see the sun go down,*
> *Nor knew till darkness that the sun was gone,*

Because our eyes were blind, while my lips drank
Oblivious love at yours.
                              But the sun sank;
Nor all our urgent wishing had the power
To lengthen out our day by one poor hour.

Then twelve years later this poem, "To the Stone Cutters":

Stone-cutters fighting time with marble, you fore-defeated
Challengers of oblivion
Eat cynical earnings, knowing rock splits, records fall down,
The square-limbed Roman letters
Scale in the thaws, wear in the rain. The poet as well
Builds his monument mockingly;
For man will be blotted out, the blithe earth die, the brave sun
Die blind and blacken to the heart:
Yet stones have stood for a thousand years, and pained thoughts found
The honey of peace in old poems.

What happened to the young bohemian athlete to make such a
radical change in what he was and how he said it? What turned the
inward eye from his own emotional preoccupations outward to the
external world of rock and stars and cyclical history? Two things,
mainly, operating on a strong and sensitive organism, conditioned
intellectually by Christianity, the classics, English romantic poetry,
and travel. Just two things: a woman, and a change of environment.

Cherchez la femme, say the French, to explain almost any situation;
and it is true that few creative men have achieved greatness without
a woman's help. Whitman's mother, Shakespeare's Dark Lady,
Browning's Elizabeth, Dante's Beatrice, Lawrence's Frieda, Yeats'
Maude and Olivia and Georgie (that wild Irishman needed three),
and Jeffers' Una—"more like a woman in a Scotch ballad," he said
of her, years later, "passionate, untamed and rather heroic—or like

a falcon—than like any ordinary person.''

They met at the University of Southern California, after Jeffers' graduation from Occidental, where Una had come from Michigan at the age of sixteen. "She had a powerful, ambitious mind," Jeffers wrote recently.

> Ambitious not for herself, but of life and knowledge. She was very beautiful, capable of intense joy and passionate resentment, little of stature, dowered with great blue eyes and heavy bronze hair. It is no wonder that she was married at seventeen.

> My first meeting with her was in a class devoted to Goethe's Faust, at the University of Southern California; for—as she told me later—she had stipulated that she must be allowed to go to college—part time—after her marriage. I have always rather disliked Goethe and his fame, thinking that Marlowe's Faustus and the Book of Job are greater poems than his great one, which derives from them. I cannot imagine why I was in that class and Una has told me that she resented my presence, because I had learned German in Europe; she had been first in the class before I joined it.

Jeffers does not describe himself as he was in 1907. In fact, he never describes himself. "Young Greek god" is the phrase said to have been applicable to him at the time he met Una.

It was six years before divorce and remarriage were possible— impassioned years of separation, travel, reckless living, and further study. Without Una, Jeffers would still have become a poet, but not the kind of poet he became. "My nature is cold and undiscriminating," he wrote. "She excited and focussed it, gave it eyes and nerves and sympathies."

For here was a marriage of educated minds as well as of beautiful young bodies, a union of two natures each incomplete and unfilled without the other. "She never saw any of my poems until they were

finished and typed," Jeffers wrote. "Yet by her presence and conversation she has co-authored every one of them. Sometimes I think
there must be some value in them if only for that reason."

The death of Una Jeffers five years ago last September ended a union
which was one of the most wonderful and creative in all literature.
The dignity with which this man has borne his loss is an example for
those to whom sorrow comes in their turn.

Una and Robin were married at Tacoma in 1913. Their plan was to
live in England and Ireland and on the Continent, but events somehow conspired to keep them in America until the following year,
when the declaration of war changed their plans forever. According
to Jeffers, ". . . the August news turned us to this village of Carmel
instead, and when the stagecoach topped the hill from Monterey,
and we looked down through pines and sea-fogs on Carmel Bay, it
was evident that we had come without knowing it to our inevitable
place."

Here then took place a second marriage, of a poet and a place, and
like his marriage with Una, this union with Carmel and the Big Sur
coast of Monterey County was lasting and productive.

Jeffers had many opportunities to wed other women and other
places, but none of them had the power to grip and to hold him.
Southern California is the setting of his first book and part of his
second; he never mentioned it again. As a region it was too dispersed,
too hot and dry, the city superficial, the coast flat. In those early
years the Malibu was closed and guarded by armed range-riders. Its
coast is reminiscent of the Big Sur. If Jeffers had been able to settle
on it . . . If . . . Pure speculation.

He settled instead at Carmel, and has lived there these forty-two
years, with a few short absences, and the poetry of his lasting fame
has been written there during uninterrupted hours each morning, on
any kind of paper at hand, line after line, poem after poem, book
upon book, the lyrics, the narratives, the adaptations of Greek tragedy which have made him world-famous.

In 1914 the Monterey coast south from Carmel was an isolated, unspoiled region, with precisely those elements needed by Jeffers to nourish his genius. Let me tell it in his own words, for this poet also writes prose of clarity, rhythm, and beauty:

> A second piece of pure accident brought us to the Monterey Coast mountains, where for the first time in my life I could see people living—amid magnificent unspoiled scenery—essentially as they did in the Idyls or the Sagas, or in Homer's Ithaca. Here was life purged of its ephemeral accretions. Men were riding after cattle, or plowing the headland, hovered by white seagulls, as they have done for thousands of years, and will for thousands of years to come. Here was contemporary life that was also permanent life; and not shut from the modern world but conscious of it and related to it; capable of expressing its spirit, but unencumbered by the mass of poetically irrelevant details and complexities that make a civilization.

Writers had come to that coast before Jeffers—Jack London, Sinclair Lewis, George Sterling, Mary Austin—and many have come since. But only Robinson Jeffers has made lasting literature from that union. It was, as he said, his inevitable place, and all the subsequent poetry he has written about it has the air of grand inevitability that is one mark of major poetry.

A point I want to make now is that Jeffers was ready for this marriage to a particular environment, as he was ready, after six years of bohemianism, for a monogamous marriage with Una. He was educated by his father and mother, by his teachers and friends in college and subsequent universities, at home and abroad. He had studied history and literature and religion and medicine, forestry and astronomy. He had Goethe's universal mind.

And so when he came to Carmel and was fired by the natural poetry around him, he was ready to deal with it, to absorb the impact of one of the most overpoweringly beautiful places on earth, and to transmute it into literature by the alchemy of art. He was trained to think and to see; he had learned the discipline of metrical rhymed verse. He could write sonnets and odes in the classical form, and he knew how to construct a tragedy according to Aristotle's *Poetics*. Lucretius, Milton, Wordsworth, and Shelley were some of his masters. No great poet has ever been hurt by education; in fact, no great poet has been uneducated. For great poetry is thought and form and style, as well as basic feeling.

The Bible was another of the master books in Jeffers' education. Some student will make a book out of the influence of the Bible on Jeffers' thought and style. He was the son of a learned Presbyterian divine. His father wanted him to be, like himself, a minister—or else a doctor. His Christian education was furthered by Occidental College. It was heartbreaking not to be able to accept the dogma. All through Jeffers' verse are expressions of sorrowful regret that he could not be what many of his friends and relatives wanted him to be. Merciless honesty is another sign of his genius. Yet there are still those who want Jeffers to be what he is not, a cheerful optimist. His view of mankind and of life developed slowly, ripened gradually, and his work was founded as true and unswerving as a Roman road; and you either take it as it is, and find strength and nourishment and direction in it, or you leave it alone. It is strong stuff, not for babes or shallow optimists—for those who would have the *Oedipus Rex* in Technicolor.

"I write verse myself," Jeffers said,

but I have no sympathy with the notion that the world owes a duty to poetry, or any other art. Poetry is not a civilizer, rather the reverse, for great poetry appeals to the most primitive instincts. It is not necessarily a moralizer; it does not necessarily improve one's character; it does not even teach good manners. It is a beautiful work of nature, like an eagle or a high sunrise. You owe it no duty. If you like it, listen to it: if not, let it alone.

I have mentioned Jeffers' knowledge of Aristotle's *Poetics*. His major narrative poems are Aristotelian in their form and purpose. Constructed after classical models, the narratives "Cawdor," "Thurso's Landing," and "Give Your Heart to the Hawks" succeed in effecting a *katharsis* on the reader, showing him the burning away of destructive emotions through pain and suffering and death, even as in life, with a corresponding relief at the end.

In spite of his rejection of Christian dogma, Jeffers is a Christian moralist. Here is what he has written, *ex post facto*, about his narrative poems:

> Besides one's duty to tell the truth and one's duty to shame the devil, it seems to me there is a third moral principle for story-tellers. The story that heaps emotions or complexities and makes no thoroughfare is a weakening story and so I should think an immoral story; but the story that through whatever passes attains significant release will influence its reader in the same sense, and this is good for him, it is moral. It is a "happy ending," for something happens, whether marriage or escape or sudden death, a lysis, a freeing of some sort; and a settlement, an adjusted balance.

As if our blood had labored all around the earth from Asia
To play its mystery before strict judges at last, the final ocean and sky...

Jeffers' shorter poems about the Monterey coast are among his happiest work, often overlooked in the excitement created by his tragic narratives and Greek adaptations, and yet they contain many elements of his genius: feeling for history and the passage of time, precise observation of the little as well as the large things in nature— for birds and flowers and rocks—and a vivid and fluent vocabulary, and a sense of form. There is a simple nobility which distinguishes his best work. Here is a short poem entitled "Bixby's Landing," about

the place where the deep canyon is now spanned by a beautiful concrete arch, and which was the setting for his long poem called
"Thurso's Landing":

They burned lime on the hill and dropped it down here in an iron car
On a long cable; here the ships warped in
And took their loads from the engine, the water is deep to the cliff. The car
Hangs half way over in the gape of the gorge,
Stationed like a north star above the peaks of the redwoods, iron perch
For the little red hawks when they cease from hovering
When they've struck prey; the spider's fling of a cable rust-glued to the pulleys.
The laborers are gone, but what a good multitude
Is here in return; the rich-lichened rock, the rose-tipped stonecrop, the constant
Ocean's voices, the cloud-lighted space.
The kilns are cold on the hill but here in the rust of the broken boiler
Quick lizards lighten, and a rattlesnake flows
Down the cracked masonry, over the crumbled fire-brick. In the rotting timbers
And roofless platforms all the free companies
Of windy grasses have root and make seed; wild buck-wheat blooms in the fat
Weather-slacked lime from the bursted barrels.
Two duckhawks darting in the sky of their cliff-hung nest are the voice of the
*   headland.*
Wine-hearted solitude, our mother the wilderness,
Men's failures are often as beautiful as men's triumphs, but your returnings
Are even more precious than your first presence.

Jeffers did not follow the path of his father. He went his own way,
true to his own vision, and what he has made as a poet was determined inevitably by what his heritage and education and life made of
him. But I would not end with my own words; I would end with his,
words charged with the magic of his own unmistakable style, sad and
strong and beautiful, possessing the unfading beauty of true poetry.
They are from the poem called "Post Mortem":

. . . and like clouds the houses
Unframe, the granite of the prime
Stand from the heaps: come storm and wash clean: the plaster is all run to the
*   sea and the steel*
All rusted; the foreland resumes
The form we loved when we saw it. Though one at the end of the age and far
*   off from this place*
Should meet my presence in a poem,
The ghost would not care but be here, long sunset shadow in the seams of the
*   granite, and forgotten*
The flesh, a spirit for the stone.

The Little Package

B y "The Little Package," of course, I mean books. And what's in
this Little Package? Dynamite, to blow you up. Honey, to heal
you. A fire opal, for beauty. A scarf of colored silk. Seashells for music. River sand to filter impurities. Rose petals. Leaves of grass.

Dynamite? A library is an explosive stockpile—all those little
packages stacked up and awaiting the detonation that occurs when
they are touched by hand and eye and mind. And when one of them
is unwrapped by the act of reading—for example, Milton's pamphlet
on the freedom of the press, the *Areopagitica*, first published in 1644
—then the fission and the fallout are more far-reaching than from any
atomic split. If you want to maintain your security and self-assurance,
stay away from certain books. Don't open that Little Package, if you
are afraid of being blown sky-high, or lulled to dreams, or dazzled by
beauty. Pandora's Box had nothing on a book.

What book? I'll name a few. Some I've lived with, read, and reread, through youth and middle age. The dangerous books are not the
ones the censors try to suppress. An honest book about sex—*Lady
Chatterley's Lover*, for example—is not dangerous, either to the individual or to society. I like that story about the Italian printer in
Florence who first set *Lady Chatterley* in type, back in 1928. Not a
word of English did he know, and when a prudish friend of his, who
did know English, warned him that the book was dangerous to mor-
als because' of what was done and the words used to tell it, the printer asked for an explanation in Italian. "My faith!" he replied. "We
do that every day!"

The dangerous books of American literature are about such things
as whales, grass, a pond in the woods, a raft on the river. Poems, es-

says, novels. Beware of these little packages, these bombs in sheep's binding. They slide down the throat, then explode in the stomach, whereas such obviously revolutionary books as *Das Kapital* and *Mein Kampf* stick in the throat, and if they are swallowed, produce indigestion from their lumpiness. Their time has passed. They are dead.

A book of poems, I said. Walt Whitman's of course. First published in 1855, in a small edition at the author's expense, with his own portrait as frontispiece, instead of his name on the title page, *Leaves of Grass* has been continuously in print for 107 years. Let me prove for you how alive it is.

Last spring at the University of California at Los Angeles, where I was university librarian and am now working as dean of the university's new School of Library Service, we were visited by twenty of the leading educators of South America. They saw everything there was to see, and as a final sight our bookish chancellor, Franklin Murphy, wanted them to see our shrine of shrines, the William Andrews Clark Memorial Library, built of marble, travertine, bronze, and oak, paid for with copper money from Montana and Arizona. The Clark Library houses the world's greatest collections of John Dryden and Oscar Wilde. Exhibits were arranged of these foreign jewels; but then just before the guests arrived I was seized by literary patriotism. Something American was needed. I rushed to the shelf and put out on a table the first edition of *Leaves of Grass* and the most beautiful modern edition of the book, the folio printed thirty years ago in San Francisco at the Grabhorn Press.

Then the guests and their wives arrived—university rectors and educators from Argentina, Chile, Uruguay, and Brazil. They strolled through the building, exclaiming at the bibliographical wonders on view—John Dryden's autograph letter to his cousin, Oscar Wilde's sad letters from prison, the first editions of *Paradise Lost* and Newton's *Principia Mathematica*. And then the Brazilian Minister of Education, an intense and restless man who had wandered after the group, with eyes glazed from too much sightseeing—Disneyland, Marineland, Forest Lawn—saw *Leaves of Grass* where I had not so innocently placed it; the little package of the first edition, the big package of the Grab-horn reprint. And, like a hawk dropping on a mouse, he fell on that book; and he came to life as though an electric current had been turned on in an idle motor. He seized the book, riffled the pages, and, finding what he was looking for, called everyone around him and began to read aloud, with a delightful accent:

> Shut not your doors to me, proud libraries,
> For that which was lacking on all your well-
>   filled shelves, yet needed most, I bring;
> The words of my book nothing—the drift of
>   it everything . . .

"He is our great poet," I said, when the Brazilian had finished.

"Ours too," he insisted. "He belongs to all the Americas. Walt Whitman should be required reading in all the schools, from the primary grades on up. What better textbook for creative living?"

He put the book down. The current went out of him, and he merged with the group.

Open the little package of a paperback Whitman, and read for yourself. If there is any life in you, the current from this book will make you spin and hum like a dynamo. If you don't react to it, you are dead and don't know it, and you will live out your deadly life exactly as surveys show most people like you to be living, subscrib-ing to the correct magazines, belonging to a book club, absorbing cultural rations along with vitamin pills, and with predigested read-ing matter in every bathroom.

But my hope is that for some few who read these words they will be a time-bomb, set to go off one year, five years, ten years hence; and then, one summer evening, such a person will be in a drugstore or a supermarket—very successful, wife or husband at home, chil-dren, cars, TV, hi-fi, magazines—and, loaded with medicants or gro-ceries, he will stop by the rack of paperbacks, and something will happen to him. At long last, these words will explode, down by his solar plexus, and in desperation he will spin the rack, seeking those books about grass and whales, about a pond in the woods, a raft on the river.

He will look around, to make sure no one sees him being different, and then he will buy *Leaves of Grass*, *Moby Dick*, *Walden*, and *Huckleberry Finn*, all for less than a fifth of Scotch. He will put them in the cart with vitamins, cold cream, and kleenex, with the nescafe, the purex, the rykrisp, and the soap that floats. He will go home with his packages of tin and paper, and their contents will be consumed— vitamins, coffee, bleach, fruit, crackers, soap—and only those littlest packages will remain. Those paperbacks. And those will be read and reread—with pencil in hand, I hope, underlining passages that move the reader to yes or no. You can do things to your own replaceable paperbacks that you can't (or shouldn't) do to library books.

In this depleting world of ours, characterized by the conventional and the orthodox, by the quickie, the cheapie, the noisy, we need, and can receive, the life and the light that are in these books. Don't ask me how. This is a miracle of chemistry, whereby the life of a creative writer is not lost when he dies, but is transfused into his book—and gives immortal vitality to *Leaves of Grass*, *Moby Dick*, *Walden*, Emerson's *Essays*, and *Huckleberry Finn*. And by another miracle, equally staggering, we can tap this life, at once explosive and consoling; can plug into this source of energy and renewal; can both dynamite and heal ourselves, merely by the act of reading.

What makes a book great, a so-called classic, is its quality of always being modern; of its author, though he be long dead, continuing to speak to each new generation.

"I have written a wicked book," Melville exulted in a letter to his neighbor Hawthorne, after completing *Moby Dick*, "and I feel spotless as the lamb."

About language, Emerson said: "The short Saxon words with which the people help themselves are better than Latin. The language of the street is always strong." In the 1850's, Emerson hailed

Whitman's vitality and vulgarity (qualities which often go together);
and I have no doubt that if Emerson were alive today, he would be
reading *Tropic of Cancer* and *The Catcher in the Rye*.

Unlike journalism, literature can never be written to order. There
is no way of foretelling the time or place of the appearance of a
masterpiece. The power of a work which elevates it from journalism
to literature shocks the conventional and scares the timid. Efforts at
censorship only serve to advertise a book. In spite of nervous parents
and self-appointed censors, *The Catcher in the Rye* has taken its place
as a kind of Bible for the present younger generation. I asked a six-
teen-year-old boy what he thought of it. "Man," he said, "I'd do all
those things Holden Caulfield did, if I only had the money!"

During the last decade I have been repeatedly in the Southwest, in
Arizona and New Mexico and the cultural parts of Texas, and always
because of books—reading, writing, collecting, and talking about
books, going with books in my baggage, books in my pocket, with
books on the seat beside me and with me in the night, best of all
companions to have and to read. Because of books I know more about
the Southwest than I could ever know by just traveling through it
and talking with people. Because of books, whenever I travel in Arizona, let us say, my companions are Kino, Garces, and Emory, on
down to Ross Santee and Joseph Wood Krutch.

When I traveled there last winter my companion was a woman, an
Army wife, Martha Summerhayes, who was in Arizona in the 1870's,
with her husband, at Forts Yuma, Mohave, Apache, Verde, Whipple,
McDowell, and Lowell, and who camped in the moonlight outside
the walls of San Xavier.

Her reminiscences of Army life were published a few years before her death in 1911, in a book called *Vanished Arizona*; and though
she died in the flesh, she lives forever in her book, reborn each time
a new edition appears, each time the book is read. When the latest
edition was published at George W. Chambers' Tucson press, Arizona Silhouettes, Raymond Carlson, editor of *Arizona Highways*, asked

me to go over Mrs. Summerhayes' trail and report on what has vanished and what remains.

Briefly, I found this: things made of perishables do not last. Wood burns, adobe melts. Flesh and blood and bone are fugitive. The barracks and stables and people of the 1870's have vanished. Books remain, however; and at Fort Mohave, although of the fort itself no trace remains. The post library is still there, if you only knew where to dig for it. In time of Indian attack, the Fort Mohave librarian buried the books and then took off. He never came back, and no one could find where he buried those books. I would rather find that library than the Lost Dutchman Mine.

In my search for the Arizona verities, on that journey, what I found unchanged was the landscape—the rivers, the desert, mountains, day sky of blue and white, night sky of black and gold. Oh yes, and the Army, God bless it! The United States Army is still there, at Fort Huachuca and the Yuma Test Station.

And books. For longer journeys, too, I have taken books with me, those little packages of American literature, and have found them good passports and good rations. Hawthorne and Hemingway, Mark Twain and Carl Sandburg and Robert Frost, Melville and Steinbeck, Emerson and J. Frank Dobie; the genteel and the vulgar, from Henry James to Henry Miller. Foreigners judge us by the books in our baggage. The timeless values these authors embody are also without national boundaries. In Africa, Asia, and India, as well as in Europe, we can go farther on paperback than in Cadillacs.

If we are to triumph in the world struggle, it will be because our ideas, not our arms, are the strongest; and books are the best packages man has ever found to hold his ideas. We should be telling the world that the American way, the revolutionary way of individual rights and freedom and responsibility, promises the fullest development for backward peoples; and the best way to tell our story is by the great books of our American heritage. Let them be translated into every tongue of mankind, printed in paperbacks, and sent down

the rivers of the world. Huck Finn and his black friend, those children of the Mississippi, will go just as surely down the Congo, the
Nile, the Ganges, and the Yellow River. Our moon travelers should
put *Walden* in their pockets; it bulks less yet weighs more than *War
and Peace*. They should hide *Huckleberry Finn* on their persons; it will
export better than *Crime and Punishment*. Even when Earth is a blue-
green cloudy ball behind us, there will need to be books in our lives,
for there is life for us in books, the essence of all the lives man has
ever lived, from Homer to Hemingway, heroic, tragic, loving,
wrapped for our convenience in this Little Package called Book.
The words of Whitman can go with us even into space:

> *I bequeathe myself to the dirt, to grow from the grass I love;*
> *If you want me again, look for me under your bootsoles.*

> *You will hardly know who I am, or what I mean;*
> *But I shall be good health to you nevertheless,*
> *And filter and fibre your blood.*

> *Failing to fetch me at first, keep encouraged;*
> *Missing me one place, search another;*
> *I stop somewhere, waiting for you.*

Bookman in Seven League Boots

MIDNIGHT-FIVE departure from Los Angeles on the third of September, a fever of lights, orchids, and languages, and finally the long runway toward the sea, as Flight 932, the DC-7 "Magnus Viking," was slowly airborne with its load of gasoline, open-face sandwiches, and people, en route to Scandinavia via the Arctic Circle. English is the cockpit and cabin language of S.A.S., an English quaintly spoken by mixed crews of Norwegians, Swedes, and Danes, with interludes in their own tongues which are and are not alike. First book out of my bag was appropriately Jespersen on the English language, which I savored throughout the twenty-two-hour flight, following his unraveling of our many-threaded tongue.

First stop was Winnipeg in the rainy dawn, oasis in a desert of wheat, fuel-stop, leg stretch, chat with a Scottish customs official, and sight of Trans-Canada's maple-leaf planes on the ground. Another long climb for altitude, followed by hours of smooth flight over pinewoods and lakeland, until the earth turned peacock blue, dappled white—Hudson's Bay with icebergs. Then we were over places with names from boyhood's geography by Carpenter, those little blue-gray books which gave one the wide world: Baffin Land, Frobisher's Island, and at sundown the autumn-colored coast of Greenland, where we made a second fuel-stop at the American airbase of Söndre Strömfjord, seeing the rust-yellow mosses and lichens that grow where the icecap has melted. Another slow climb with a fresh load of gasoline and sandwiches, and then we were over another kind of desert, the great icecap, rose-blue in the last light, pierced by crevasses into which were falling rivulets of melt, then into the cloud-cap as night fell.

We made dawn landing at Copenhagen, after a majestic sweep over the harbor, welcomed by a rising cloud of gulls and escorted to the center of town by a parade of cyclists. Paris of the North? A tidier version, more fastidious, as witnessed by the quality of the street-workers, gastronomically grosser, somewhat to Paris what San Francisco is to New York, lacking the enormous vitality which comes from size. While waiting for our hotel room to be readied, we eased stiffness by walking to Frascati's for breakfast, and then took a bus and boat tour of the city. Nothing gives soul to a city as water does, whether it be sea-town, lake-city, or river-port. The boat stopped for tourists to take pictures of the Little Mermaid. Preferring a direct vision of life, we carried no kodak, and so we gazed at the statue with our eyes, while the others looked at her with their cameras. *Bon mot* of the tour came from the multi-lingual guide, who referred to Copenhagen's newest hotel, the tall thin Europa, as a "tourist silo." Ours was a small hotel in the Nielshemingsgade, whose only disadvantage was in being opposite the Church of the Holy Ghost, with bells that rang the quarter-hours around the clock. We were up high enough to see midnight fireworks on the closing day of the Tivoli Gardens' summer season.

One evening, after a better than good dinner at Krog's Fish Restaurant, we walked past the squat statue of the aproned Fish Wife, as beautiful in her way as the Little Mermaid, and on to the waterfront where we saw the night boats to Aarhus and Malmö being readied, and a freighter swinging out cases of empty Carlsberg and Tuborg bottles, and full drums of whale oil.

The next morning we crossed Town Hall Square as crowds cheered the arrival of the king and queen of Denmark and the president of Finland to call on the mayor of Copenhagen. We wormed to a vantage point and stood for an hour until the royal couple and guest emerged, smiled and waved, and were swallowed by a Bentley.

The university quarter, with its bookshops and restaurants and paired students, made me nostalgic for my student years in France.

Here I extended my Danish education, commenced earlier by Knud Merrild, Jens Nyholm, Waldemar Westergaard, and Jean Hersholt, by good food and talk with librarians Preben Kirkegaard, Ole Jacobsen, and Carl Thomsen, literate spokesmen for all that we hold good and true. In a restaurant we heard radio music from Helsinki upon the death of Sibelius.

Copenhagen is rich in memorials to Scandinavia's great, other than the Storyteller. A plaque on the wall near the Faculty of Letters told that Holberg had lived there, 1740-1754, while he taught at the university. In the rose garden at the Royal Library we paid homage to a statue of Søren Kierkegaard, glistening in the rain. Sheltered in the library, one of Europe's great research collections, we were graciously toured by Assistant Librarian Magnussen in the absence of Royal Librarian Palle Birkelund, moved as always by sight of readers fused with the books and manuscripts they were holding, breathing that sweet smell of old books which permeated the erstwhile fortress building. Passing the newspaper stack we saw an old man hopping about like a squirrel after nuts, and were told that he was one of Denmark's eminent scholars, far into his eighties, and one of the few persons allowed the run of the library because of his vast knowledge of what and where. Here in this library where his manuscripts are preserved, I thought of Bishop Grundtvig, who revolutionized Danish education by insisting on the personality of the teacher as being more important than a pedantic curriculum—a revolution needed in the United States where theory, method, and certification are bulldozing the life of education.

The new public library in downtown Copenhagen shares a building with the Ministry for Greenland, and as I entered and looked about admiringly and inquiringly at the fresh decor, I was welcomed and oriented by the coatroom girl. In the literature room I peeked at an oblivious old man's book. It was Zane Grey's *Union Pacific*, in English.

We departed from Copenhagen's airport on a rainy morning, and I was sorely tempted to play hooky from schedule and hop to Aarhus, capital of Jutland, that seagirt peninsula from whence comes much of Denmark's strength and sensitivity, remembering a Christmas present in 1945 from Jens Jutlander—a copy of *The Jutland Wind*, a translation of verse from the peninsula. As in all European airports, the intercontinental flights being called also were powerfully seductive —most of all Stockholm, Copenhagen, Frankfort, Rome, Athens, and Khartoum, terminating in Nairobi.

"I should have liked to rise and go, where the golden apples grow," but instead we went on S.A.S. Flight 561 to London, flying above broken overcast with glimpses of green fields and red roofs, clearing as we crossed the North Sea. We landed at London Airport on a gala Sunday afternoon, crowds lining the promenades to watch the planes come and go—Vickers Viscounts of B.E.A., a Convair of Aer Lingus, Douglas and Lockheed planes of the American lines and Air France, and our first sight of a Bristol Britannia of B.O.A.C.

Rolling in to Waterloo air terminal on a B.E.A. bus, I felt that the rhythm of London had not changed, even with traffic at its worst— as, for example, at Hammersmith Broadway, Shepherd's Bush Roundabout, or the Hyde Park Corner. The vehicles at those maelstroms are conducted in a well-mannered and dignified way, compared with New York or Paris.

Seven years earlier we had lived in a Chelsea flat, and though only ten minutes from the heart of London, it was like living in a suburb, up in high rooms overlooking the river and the hills of Kent and Surrey. Now on this briefer stay we lodged at Brown's Hotel in Dover-Albemarle Streets, just off Piccadilly, one of London's most quietly elegant hotels with long bathtubs, soft water, and castile soap. The food was English, the service ritualized; one adapts or starves. Beef had returned to the menu. No more of 1950's reindeer.

For a few weeks bookshops were my haunt, as I sought to do in that time what had taken me a year before. My efforts culminated in the purchase for the state-wide University of California libraries of the eighty-thousand-volume library left by C.K. Ogden, the eccentric scholar who devised Basic English.

Tweed cap, cashmere sweater, Viyella shirts, Church shoes, and a Jaguar fitted me for the road, while my wife collected little handmade woolen birds and beasts to take to all the children at home. We wondered what the maid thought one evening when she came to turn down our beds and found them a menagerie!

The Great North Road from London to Edinburgh is too narrow for the traffic it carries. Although lorry drivers are careful, their number makes speed impossible. There was no hurry. In mid-September frost had not yet blackened the dahlias. There were yellow fields of mustard. Men with chopping knives were waging their ancient war on the encroaching hedges, swinging savagely at the tough stems. Through the hedges crept blackberry vines whose ripe fruit people sought with cautious fingers. Virginia creeper on walls had turned red. Leaves had not yet begun to fall, though beeches were yellowing.

Our itinerary included cathedrals and bookshops. St. Albans was a dark freeze, wherein we found the tomb of Bernard de Mandeville, the Elizabethan traveler. Yews in the churchyard were old and beautiful. Elsewhere in town friends lunched us on lamb, green beans, and apple pie, and sold me a great collection of books on early English education. From booksellers near Cambridge I bought such varieties as British detective fiction and a limestone sculpture by Eric Gill. In Oxford we revisited Christ Church to see the John Evelyn collection arranged by Deputy Librarian Hiscock. At Newbury we stayed with friends, and while the girls did more than talk about food, the man and I, snug from rain in his garden bookroom, sold and bought books—a great collection of English novels of three centuries and Scottish imprints of the 1600's—happy in one of the best of all symbiotic relationships, that of bookseller and librarian.

On the way north it was too rainy to stop in Peterborough, and we passed through with only a glimpse of the tree-girt Norman abbey.

Lincoln was rainy, but we were cozy under the tight roof of the Royal Saracen's Head, and in the misty morning trudged up Steep Hill to see the cathedral on its airy site, with lacy façade and immaculate close, dominated by a statue of Tennyson. We entered as the choir was singing matins, filling the vast space with heavenly sound; saw the Lincoln Imp; and departed. In a bookshop I sought vainly for Lawrence's *Rainbow*, wanting to reread the chapter called "The Cathedral." It was not until we returned to London that I found a copy. Alas, the chapter was more about the inside of Lawrence than of Lincoln.

On the outskirts of York a level-crossing gate arrested us for the passage of a train; and presently it came, running fast in the rain, trailing clouds of steam; not *a* train, but rather The Flying Scotsman, making the four-hundred-mile London-Edinburgh run in eight hours, its red and cream coaches drawn by a black, green, and gold engine named "Sir Nigel Healey," beautiful apparition no sooner seen than gone, swallowed up in the mist, leaving the echo of its banshee whistle.

York meant Scotch broth and a fluffy omelet, a rare Duchess of Newcastle imprint found in a shop in the Stonegate, the apple-green glass of the Minster—and rain. Memorable was a visit to the ruins of Fountains Abbey, the medieval Cistercian monastery near Harrogate, on a clear mild day toward long-shadowed evening after all the trippers had gone, leaving the skeleton arches to the rooks and us. The black birds rose and settled and rose again in raucous protest as we walked on the grass, which grew where once lay flagstone floors. Sheep grazed. I sensed many silent sacred presences, and thought of Browning's "Love Among the Ruins":

> *Where the quiet-coloured end of evening*
> > *smiles*
> > > *Miles and miles*
> *On the solitary pastures where our sheep*

Half-asleep
Tinkle homeward thro' the twilight
stray or stop
As they crop—

North to the Border the country begins to thin out and depeople itself, giving a Southwestern-American the feeling he gets on approaching his homeland, after exile in the East and Midwest. Stones take the place of shrubs as hedgerow material; hills are domed and barren and given over to sheep; and the Tyne, though by no means an *arroyo seco*, flows sparingly over golden stones as it nears Newcastle and smoke-veiled marriage with salt water. On the grass along the river, white chickens were scattered like confetti. At the Wellington, in a village called Riding Mill, we had one of the best lunches in Britain: lightly fried filet of sole, parsleyed potatoes, a slice of lemon, and ginger beer.

Across river near Corbridge, under High Brunton in a meadow edged with beeches, we found one of the remaining sections of the Roman Wall, built by the Emperor Hadrian about 120 A.D., a strong point called Brunton Turret, preserved as a national monument: a hundred feet long, five feet thick and as many high, a mass of brute masonry mortared in till doomsday.

Southbound through the Lake Country we paused overnight at Windermere, finding too many people and not enough country. It was like a city park. Windermere's tributaries were nice, though, pouring out of the hillsides clear and cold, and so was the local building stone, all green slate. The Lake Poets were lost in the remembrance that Beatrix Potter lived and died on her sheep farm across the lake. At this stage of experience I would be tempted to trade Wordsworth for *The Tale of Peter Rabbit* and Coleridge for *Squirrel Nutkin*, with Southey thrown in for *The Tale of Jemima Puddleduck*.

Forging southward through the gauntlet of Liverpool and Birmingham, newly partial to Lawrence's hatred of industrialism, we gained sanctuary in County Shropshire, took tea in Shrewsbury, then crossed sodden fields and the swollen Severn at Worcester. Darkness had fallen when we reached our destination, the village of Broadway in the Cotswolds and one of England's loveliest inns, the Lygon Arms, constructed of the yellow local limestone, continuously a hostelry since the time of Shakespeare. Added since, however, were such amenities as running hot water, lighter fare, and the English equivalent of Beautyrest mattresses.

Late that afternoon, sight of the wooded hill known as Wenlock Edge had evoked the *Shropshire Lad* and Vaughan Williams' setting of Housman's poems, in the song cycle for tenor and string quartet called *On Wenlock Edge*, and a longing to hear that music again.

> *On Wenlock Edge the wood's in trouble;*
> *His forest fleece the Wrekin heaves;*
> *The gale, it plies the saplings double,*
> *And thick on Severn snow the leaves.*

The Lord was good to us, for back in London a few days later hear it we did, at one of the great concerts of our life, held in the honeycomb Royal Festival Hall in honor of Vaughan Williams' eighty-fifth birthday—and that oak of a man was there to hear his music and to bless an overflow crowd, including students in turtle-necks and slacks, fully as good to watch in their relaxed mood as the music was to hear. Basil Cameron conducted the *Pastoral Symphony*, *Job, A Masque for Dancing*, and the song cycle, rearranged for orchestra to accompany the tenor voice. Williams' shadow-dappled music *is* the English countryside and character, as the music of Sibelius typifies Finland.

Emerging into the damp blue murk, seeing barge lights on the river, and hearing Big Ben strike ten, I had the impression of a Whistler Nocturne. My only regret was that the program had not included the *London Symphony*, Williams' early work which transmuted impressions of the city into music more lasting perhaps even than London itself.

The distance between London and Paris is no measure of the gulf between the two ways of life. The airport limousines of British European Airways and Air France typify the differences. The ride from the Cromwell Road terminal to London Airport was as solemn as the last ride in a hearse. Twenty miles an hour. Silent driver. Passengers whispering, if they spoke at all.

Then the swift flight on B.E.A.'s 333, a Vickers Viscount, to Le Bourget and a spreading sense of irresponsibility on the part of employees and passengers. Yet somehow the bus was boarded and away we went, full speed on hard tires over cobbled streets, the driver shouting to no one in particular, the passengers screaming to be heard above rattling windows and doors. The streets had not been cleaned in years, and we left a wake of leaves, papers, trash, and angry cyclists. It was like a caricature by Dubout. A difference also in taxis, with the square and commodious London type succeeded by small cars unable comfortably to accommodate either people or luggage, and driven by apache types.

It was a day or two before the charm of Paris began to work, so different is it from London's magic to which we had become accustomed. Composed of smells, sights, and sounds, the charm of Paris is irresistible, though one is repelled at first by an initial impression of brutality and a price for everything. This is why Henry Miller's *Tropic of Cancer* is a great book, banned though it be in the English-speaking countries, so perfectly does it embody the *ambiance* of Paris unbuttoned.

We lodged in a doll-size hotel on the Quai Saint-Michel, overlooking the bookstalls, the Seine, the Palaces of Commerce and Justice, and Notre Dame, gloriously floodlit at night. Traffic on the street below had only two tempos around the clock: stand-still for red light, full-speed for green. Parisians once drove with their horns; now throttles do it. Half a block away the Place Saint-Michel boiled

with student life. A walk up boulevard to the Sorbonne was like running the rapids of the Colorado in reverse. No color line. The blacker
the man's skin, the blonder the girl. A sense of youth's blind vitality.
Be-bops the modern *fauves*. Immemorial atmosphere of freedom within the restraints of custom.

Up hill we took sanctuary in the Pantheon and saw the pastel murals of Puvis de Chavannes, delicate as the music of Debussy. We
reached the Luxembourg Garden at closing time and watched people
of all ages shuffling out through rainbow leaves, herded by a gendarme
with lock and key and thirst for an *apéritif*. Big-leafed chestnuts were
towers of gold. Little-leafed trees launched their relics like yellow
butterflies. The ground was carpeted. No one raked, no one burned.

Choice of eating places in Paris is nearly limitless among the four
thousand restaurants in the city. Whatever the choice, there was always *soup du jour* of potato, leek, carrot, turnip, or spinach, a meal in
itself, served family style. *Choucroute garnie* at Brasserie Lipp. *Omelette
aux champignons* at Calvert next door. *Filet de boeuf charolais* at the
Relais de St. Germain, tender and succulent, garnished with water-
cress, hemmed with wild rice and chopped mushrooms. A steak to
end steaks at the Brasserie Perigourdine on the night of the general
strike, when only those restaurants with charcoal were able to serve.
Poisson dorade, a kind of Mediterranean goldfish, Chez Josephine,
followed by coffee at the Closerie des Lilas, in an atmosphere of deep
peace, polished brass, mahogany walls, marble-top tables, and leather
seats, with the habitués—man with poodle, a couple reading Camus
together, chess players, poet in the throes of creation, there in the
café on the edge of Montparnasse, once a country inn, the Lilac Farm,
on the road to Orléans.

Paris in the fall, dirty, bittersweet, fatal, all things to all people
regardless of age, sex, or purse, city of light and lust. Along the Quai
des Orfèvres grow tall elms, and one looks up at blue sky through a
filigree of golden leaves, while down below he sees barges on the
river, bearing master, wife, children, dogs, and the family washing

on a deck-line. And sees the eternal fishermen who catch nought. The bookstalls fascinated my wife—not their trite contents, but rather the men and women who ran them and the people who browsed and sometimes bought. Day's end was the best time for sales, she observed.

One cloudy day, sans electricity, gas, transportation, and (most critical of all) morning coffee, we trudged up river to the Jardin des Plantes, and found its denizens indifferent to the strike of workers, as well as to us. This was the zoo where Rilke walked alone, half a century before, conceiving poems to its flamingoes and panthers.

> His sight from ever gazing through the bars has grown so blunt
> that it sees nothing more. It seems to him that thousands of bars
> are before him, and behind them nothing merely.

Toward noon we found ourselves on the Cité across from our *quai*, in the Brasserie des Deux Palais opposite the Sainte Chapelle. There by some culinary miracle we were served eggs on ham, crusty sweet-buttered bread, and coffee *almost* hot. Thus heartened we continued our walk, through the Louvre and the Tuileries Gardens, seeing the bust of Le Notre (1634-1700), designer of the Tuileries and all of France's classic parks, on to the Place de la Concorde and up the Rue Royale to the Madeleine and the flower stands along its flank. Here in 1849 Chopin had been given a great funeral. "Play Mozart," he said on his deathbed, "and I will hear you." They sang the *Requiem*, K. 626.

On a day of flying clouds we went by train to Chartres. This time, as my wife raised her eyes to the windows, I cast mine to the floor, observing its worn softness, warm to the eye, cold to the hand, laid to outlast all the feet in the world. I wanted to take her to the restaurant where years before I had seen the Great God Pan, disguised as a cheese-peddling shepherd, but feared that potent deity had long since departed. In our hunger was memory of that meal at the Relais de St. Germain; we rushed back to Paris and fell on a two-thirty lunch of soup, fish, salad, and fruit, a meal which lasted till four o'clock. Lovely day!

Another trip was to Dijon one morning from the Gare de Lyon, on a *rapide* made up of through cars to Bern, Geneva, Lyon, Marseilles, Nice, and Italy, the split-up to occur at Dijon. We took red plush seats in an Italian coach destined for Milano and observed the stream of travelers, anxiously seeking the cars of their destinations. The members of a symphony orchestra on tour arrived late, protecting an assortment of instruments from the rain. At eight-ten the train soundlessly followed the electric engine out of the station on the three-hour nonstop run to Dijon, two hundred miles southeast. Rain followed us, and we looked through its curtain on brown fields and yellow woods, on shining red-roofed villages, and finally on the hills of Burgundy, with a glimpse at Alésia of the heroic statue of Vercingetorix, last of the Gallic chieftains to capitulate to Caesar, here on the plain, in the year 52 B.C.

A rainy Dijon underlined Victor Hugo's description of the Burgundian capital: *délicieuse ville, mélancolique et douce*. My last sight of her golden towers had been on a May afternoon. Now the limestone was drab, as I sought the scenes of my student days, a quarter-century before. Huddled under a single umbrella we trudged the cobbled streets, past the home shop of Grey-Poupon mustard, the Patisserie Michelin which baked the flakiest of goodies, the Restaurant Racouchot, *Aux Trois Faisans*, statues of the Grape Treader, of Rameau, Bossuet, and Rude. In the four-storied building of the Faculté des Lettres where, twenty-five years ago to the month, I had faced the jury in defense of my thesis and been awarded the Doctorate of the University of Dijon, students were jammed and the foyer stank of wet wool. Down the narrow Rue du Petit-Potet we splashed to the pension at Number 14 where I had lived, neighbor to the mayor of Dijon and the bishop of Burgundy, though with medieval plumbing. The limestone was lifeless, the cobbles rough, the rain cold; the only color was of the multihued tile roofs.

We took shelter in the museum, quartered in a wing of the Hotel de Ville, the former ducal palace, and found it refurbished by a new director, the inner sanctum occupied, as of yore, by the tombs of the dukes and their wives, the masterpiece of the Flemish sculptor, a bronze statue of whom by Rude stood in the courtyard, austere, aproned, chisel and hammer in hand, indifferent to the incessant rain. *Claus Sluter, Imagier aux Ducs de Bourgogne*, read the inscription on the base.

In the Place Darcy at the opposite end of the Rue de la Liberté from the museum, we again sheltered, in the Café de la Concorde where on the banquette, under gilt-framed mirrors, we took *thé anglais*, served by a flatfooted *garçon* whom I recognized from student years. In answer to my question as to how long he had served there, he replied, *Thirty-seven years*. Next to us bridge-playing Dijonnais drank beer and conversed in the hoarse patois of Burgundy. A table of matrons sipped hot chocolate. A lone man wrote a letter on café stationery. Another read *Le Bien Public*. Nothing had changed. Only I.

Back up the hill past the Hotel de la Cloche we walked through sodden leaves to our hosts' home overlooking Dijon. We were staying with Docteur Georges Connes and his wife and daughter. This was the man under whom I had studied, the learned and tolerant professor of English language and literature, dean of the Faculty of Letters, Resistance hero, mayor of Dijon, now in retirement, dividing his time between Dijon and his ancestral farm far south in the mountainous Rouergue. In his attic study under the rain-pattered shingles, he showed me the work he was doing on the local history of the Rouergue, based on family papers of several centuries, and the major work that had occupied his free time during the Occupation— the first French translation of Browning's *The Ring and the Book*.

Snapshots he showed me portrayed incidents of the Liberation when, in spite of Mayor Connes' efforts, the populace had dealt direct justice by hanging from a lamppost in the Place d'Armes the commissioner of police who had collaborated with the Nazis, and patriots had seized, stripped, and shaved the heads of several women of *mauvaise vie*.

The next morning was clear, and we drove around town in Connes' tiny open-topped Citroën. We saw the new Faculty of Sciences building on the outskirts of town and enormous new apartment houses. The monument to patriots executed by the Nazis was impressive: simply the rifle range, with the heroes' names carved on the wall before which they had fallen. One hundred thirty-four of them.

Down the Côte d'Or toward Beaune we drove, seeing the vineyards after the vintage, golden with an occasional red clump, now open to gleaners. Growing on the eastern slopes of the limestone hills and extending a short way onto the plain, the vineyards of the red Burgundies unrolled like the wine list in a restaurant: Clos Vougeot, Corton, Romanée, Chambertin. In the village of Gevrey Chambertin we saw the graveyard where Gaston Roupnel is buried, the old hawk-faced professor of Burgundian folklore whose lectures I had followed, a novelist whose *Nono, or the Life of the Soil* was translated into English.

We returned to Paris on the four-thirty *rapide* from Marseilles, St. Etienne, and Lyon, boarding a section which came in from Besançon to be coupled to the main train. Another nonstop run, through fields and woods, along rivers and canals, seeing an occasional hunter with gun and dog, as darkness fell and crows came to roost, through a countryside unchanged in a thousand years.

Seven-thirty arrival at Gare de Lyon allowed sight of the Simplon-Orient Express drawn up on the next track for eight o'clock departure to Trieste, Belgrade, Bucharest, Athens, and Istanbul, via Dijon, Geneva, and the Simplon Tunnel through the Alps. On another track stood the Blue Train on which we had once ridden to Nice. We took the Metro to the Place Saint-Michel and our hotel. It was like coming home. We had grown accustomed to the noise and to the street light which the drawn curtain failed to dim. Dinner was anti-gastronomical: fruit in our room.

The next day we made a rainy flight to Amsterdam on a K. L. M. Convair. Across the aisle a Dutch burgher returned from holiday with a bird-cage and a bottle of cognac. We lodged in a friend's eighteenth-century bookshop-apartment on the Keizersgracht Canal, with a view onto a secluded garden. The rain it raineth every day in Amsterdam, and we were content to spend hours in talk with friends. The coffee shops serve rich pastries, thick cream, and coffee. Barrel organs drown out the noise of traffic. We came upon a hidden square of seventeenth-century pensioners' houses, overlooking a greensward and a statue of the gentle Jesus. Restaurants in town and country contributed to our sense of well-fed-being. We saw one windmill. Books bought included a collection of printing by Bodoni of Parma and a 1672 Dutch translation of Donne's poetry.

Wonderful was a visit to the Ryksmuseum and sight of the Rembrandts, alive with lights and shadows. The self-portraits at thirty and sixty are heartbreaking testimonials to what he acknowledged life had done to him, almost too painful to contemplate. To sit before them was to sit to Rembrandt himself, the three centuries since his passing telescoped into an eternal present.

As we left the museum rain began to fall and we ran the short distance to our abode on the Keizersgracht, and that night at dinner with twenty booksellers and the university librarian I wished for a Rembrandt to immortalize a meeting of deep understanding and good will.

An eleven o'clock departure found us dining earlier with our hosts, looking out on the rainy concourse where the Flying Dutchmen of K.L.M. were coming and going to and from the ends of the earth. We boarded our DC-7 in the rain and were airborne nonstop for New York. Over England weather cleared and we saw the lights of Manchester, and later those of Dublin, like a golden hive in swarm. Then all through the night nothing but moonlit ocean and broken clouds, landfall at Newfoundland, thence down coast to an easy landing Idlewild.

Our car had arrived on the freighter *American Scout* the day before.

My wife flew on home, leaving me to drive across country alone, an experience I had relished in 1951. "First catch your Jaguar." It took me several days of misplaced papers, broken choke, and other human and mechanical delays to get the car unloaded, through customs, off dock, and over to Long Island for servicing. When I finally got behind the wheel of the sleek gray car and slipped into evening traffic, gained the Queens Midtown Bridge, crossed Manhattan, took the Lincoln Tunnel under the Hudson, and headed south on the New Jersey Turnpike toward Los Angeles and way points, my exultation was boundless. The car ran like a watch. The radio was alive with all kinds of music. At the first Howard Johnson's I savored a plate of scallops, then drove on to the Pennsylvania Turnpike and west to Willow Springs, north of Philadelphia, where I bedded for the night.

The next day we ate up 375 miles of autumn-colored Appalachians, reached the Ohio Turnpike, then angled southwest to sleep in Columbus. Along the roads baskets of apples were for sale, but when I ordered applesauce for breakfast, it came from a can. Stops at Earlham College and at the University of Illinois slowed me a bit, but then I reached U.S. 54, on its great diagonal traject from Chicago to El Paso, crossed the Mississippi at the river town of Louisiana, the Missouri at Jefferson City, through the sere Ozarks and dropped onto the stubble fields of Kansas, leaving behind a swirl of dead leaves. In towns and villages old people were raking and burning. The car gathered the sweet smell of the smoke as I rolled southwestward. Once beside a field of dead corn, I listened to the dry rustle—music never heard in my homeland.

Weather worsened as I quit Kansas for Oklahoma, Texas, and New Mexico—rain turning to snow. Still the car ran smoothly, its heater keeping me warm, the radio never on the same station for long. I heard a faculty wives' orchestra play Mozart beautifully. Recipes for cooking broccoli. An illustrated lecture on César Franck's mastery of the canon form. All about job opportunities in Wichita. I kept rolling. Cows in the dead corn, golden ears cribbed. It was late in the year for autumn colors, but an occasional maple with the sun shining through was a breath-catching *luminario*. Sputnik II kept lapping the Jaguar in spite of my haste. At Tucumcari I left 54 for 66, crossed the Sandias in a snowstorm, and descended to Albuquerque in a burst of sundown light.

The rest of the way, a mere eight hundred miles, was home country, nothing foreign in the color and configuration of the landscape, all mountains mapped and known—Taylor, Graham, Mingus, and finally, across desert and river and desert again, Cuyamaca, Old Saddleback, and the Santa Monicas of Southern California. Here was autumn too, the year fallen, apparent only to those with loving eyes.

In Search of Spring

IT was a big road sign bearing two roads: ARLBERG and BRENNER. We took the Brenner turn to the left and in a few minutes, as we left the valley floor, Innsbruck disappeared in the rain. The rain turned to sleet as we climbed toward the pass, then to snow.

The road was two-lane, heavily traveled in both directions. Descending toward Austria were huge diesel trucks loaded with logs; ascending toward Italy trucks and passenger vehicles of many nations. Their wheels kept the snow from staying on the road, so the pavement was wet and firm. Traffic and poor visibility were my problems, and I did no sightseeing. My wife reported Christmas trees on both sides of the road, a railroad track, a chasm. Tightened seat belts gave us a sense of security.

This was the Brenner Pass, ancient route through the Alps, a comparatively low, wide pass kept open year around, not like the high and narrow Arlberg we had come over earlier, barely making it through ice and snow. I kept the Porsche in third and second gears, finding it sure-wheeled, swift, and flexible, slipping in and out of traffic holes, adding to my wife's gray hairs.

BRENNERO at the summit meant Italy, immigration and customs, and sight of a long train, the Rome-Munich Express, pulling out northbound. All the while light snow was falling, and spring seemed far away. And then we were descending, the road still narrow and clotted with traffic, the weather the reverse of the Austrian side— snow to sleet to rain; and finally the end of the weather front, and the snowy Dolomites towering on both sides of the canyon road. The architecture had changed from wood to stucco. Castles occupied many of the high points. Terraced orchards of fruit trees were still leafless. The air was cold, the car warm and snug, as we dropped fast in third gear, the ruby-red car like a hummingbird in and out of the traffic stream.

At twilight and 275 miles from the morning's start in Salzburg, we reached Trento. Almost without steering, the car found its way to the courtyard of the Gran Hotel, bounded by the pollarded plane trees.

It was indeed a *grand* hotel, a lobby with marble floor and pillars, a long reception desk at which a formally-dressed concierge received us with a sepulchral "Buono sera." He *was* a creepy one, tall, gaunt, waxlike, a character out of a Gothic novel; and apparently the only other human there. He led us to a faraway room, also with a marble floor, huge beds, and red velvet drapes; and there we stayed, making supper of biscuits, dried fruit, and a Swiss chocolate bar, in a setting that recalled one in *A Farewell to Arms*.

The next day was Sunday. We were down for early breakfast in a marble dining room. The waiter was not the concierge, but he too was Gothic. While we breakfasted with rolls, jam, butter, and poor coffee, he stood at attention and watched us eat. "We must be the first guests this year," I whispered. "Tell him to go away," my wife replied, "and bring us some really hot coffee."

It didn't seem advisable to disturb the waiter's vigil. We crept by him, packed, and I carried our bags down and paid the concierge. He helped me load the car and bowed low as we sped out of Trento, heading down the widening limestone valley through orchards and vineyards, seeing village groups of black-garbed men in earnest discussion, of politics, probably, rather than religion. The river whose valley we were descending was the Adigi, which we had followed all the way from Bolzano below Brennero. To the west, over the mountains lay the Lago di Garda; and at Verona where the valley widened out into the Lombardy plain, we reached a point of decision. Over cappuccino in a café, we studied the map. Here was the *autostrada* which led east to Padova and Venezia, west to Brescia, Milano, and Torino.

If we crossed it and continued south over the plain to Mantova and Parma, we would reach the Autostrada del Sole, Italy's great new freeway, which ran from Milano to Firenze.

It was good to be aimless, free to go where fancy led, a rare thing in our middle-aged lives. A second cup brought the decision to push on to Florence. We had good memories of that city. I had lived there once thirty years ago. Fay remembered its jeweled galleries from a tour in her teens.

On across the plain we sped, as spring began to appear. Fruit trees were in flower, fields were green, poplars and mulberries had leafed out, rivers were running high. The Po was at flood stage, the bridge out, and we crossed the wild brown water on planks laid on boats lashed together. Then at Reggio nell' Emelia we entered the *autostrada*. The Porsche responded with a burst of speed that carried us a hundred miles, over the plain and through the Apennines. At the summit we encountered more snow, then rain, and finally the springtime beauty of Tuscany, the olive trees like green smoke on the hills, the pastel stuccos set in orchards of flowering fruit and nut trees, forming the immemorial landscape of the Renaissance painters.

After long absence I managed nevertheless to gain town center and beyond to the Lungarno Zecca where we found lodging in a comfortable hotel on the riverbank. Faithful restoration had been made of the damage suffered when the Germans withdrew; the new Ponte Santa Trinita, the world's most beautiful bridge, was a perfect replica of the old.

After a bath we walked through the teeming streets to the Duomo, Giotto's Tower, and the Baptistery, and found the latter in working order. Two newborn babies, warmly wrapped and lovingly held by peasant parents, were being baptized in the deep-freeze interior, by a priest wearing hat and overcoat.

Then we found the café where I used to read Joyce, drink a *piccola birra*, and watch Europe's fairest women go by; and there we sat for an hour over a cappuccino, immersed in waves of talk, social, political, literary, impassioned whatever the subject, the expressive faces and hands of the talkers a joy to watch.

It was easy to linger in Florence. We left the car in the garage and walked everywhere. The museums were cold and poorly lit. In the Riccardi Palace a guide held a spotlight on Gozzoli's golden murals. On the Ponte Vecchio we shopped for gold and silver and enamel gifts. At Sabatini's we savored a cream of spinach soup, *scampi pescatori*, zucchini salad, pineapple and cream, in one of the best meals of the trip, deliciously cooked, graciously served.

I tried in vain to find my old pensione, the Crocini, on the Lungarno Guicciardini. Gone. Perhaps a war casualty. The riverbanks had suffered heavy damage. Behind the Pitti Palace we toiled up paths and stairs to the top of the Boboli Gardens, then looked out over the sea of buff and rose-colored walls and roofs, the brown river, the dark green cypresses and pines, and across to Fiesole and the Apennines. At Alinari's we bought Christmas cards, a print of Mozart in the Bologna Academy; in the market at the Piazza della Signoria an orange-colored raffia hat for Fay, in the English pharmacy American razor blades for me. Dante, Ruskin, Browning, and Landor, Hare, Pater, and Sean O'Faolain were at our side, as I recalled things they had written about Florence.

On the expressway to the sea we arrowed through to the coast above Livorno, and then we began a long journey around the Mediterranean shore that would take us all the way to Valencia, following at first a flat beach, groved by umbrella pines, then cutting inland at Spezia where the great cliffs are impassable, finding the Porsche an agile contender among the competitive Italian drivers. I stopped in answer to one driver's hail. He proved to be a smuggler, a sailor from an Ecuadorian freighter, who offered us assorted contraband—woolens, perfumes, radios. I sped away and left him with his wares unsold.

Later a decenter sort flagged us down. "Schweiz?" he asked in German, pointing to our license plates. I replied in French, he countered in English, then tested my Italian, and I tried my Spanish. A homesick Zuricher, he advised us, wisely as it turned out, where to stay for the night at Alassio, beyond Genoa.

Then we descended again to a postcard-blue sea and followed a corniche road steeply terraced with rock walls of great age and beauty, planted with old olives, rising above us, tended by hand, each particle of earth and manure carried up in baskets and distributed among the trees. For miles we followed this beautiful road, through Rapallo with its memories of Beerbohm, Pound, and Yeats, then gained the swarming waterfront of Genoa, and finally reached Alassio as darkness fell, where we ate and slept well to the gentle wash of water on the pebbled shore.

The next morning we traversed the flower coast of the Italian Riviera, seeing as many terraces of carnations as of olives on the day before. In San Remo we stopped for cappuccino, and Fay allowed as how she could settle there gladly and spend the rest of her days among the flowers.

On we pressed, however, across the frontier at Ventimiglia, where I had once been plucked off a train because of having no French visa, and on to Nice and lodging at the grand old Hotel Ruhl, No. 1 Promenade des Anglais, where we had stayed for the UNESCO Conference in 1950. Again a huge bedroom and bath, and again we made our way to the Café Monot on the Place Masséna for local dishes: *salade niçoise*, *omelette provençale*, grilled *loup de mer* seasoned with fennel.

And again it rained throughout our stay in Nice, as it had thirteen years before, a cold rain off the snowy Alps. The flower market was held regardless and we splashed and huddled and reveled in the smells and colors and voluble excitement of buyers and sellers. Another day we dawdled back and forth along the three corniche roads, to Monte Carlo and back for lunch on the waterfront at Villefranche: *petite friture*, heaping plates of crisp fishlets; and watched the next table all but founder in a huge bouillebaisse. In the old port of Nice we saw the white cruise ship *Meteor* out of Bergen for Cagliari, and I came out second best when, unsure of the flag she was flying, I hailed the deck officer.

"Are you British?"

"No, Norwegian."

"Sorry," I replied.

"I'm not," he shot back.

She was a beauty, as she backed out under her own power, cleared the breakwater, and headed straight out toward Sardinia.

Our stay in Nice was only until I could get the car serviced, and then we headed west on the new autoroute that bypassed Cannes, back of the Esterels, coming out into a landscape pure Cézanne. And why not? This was Aix-en-Provence where he lived and painted, a countryside not unlike southern California, at least that part around Hemet—San Jacinto.

We lunched at the Nord-Pinus in Arles, a Sunday lunch in a bourgeois setting Flaubert would have relished for its "copy," then crossed the Rhone and the Petite Rhone, over the Camargue delta, sidetripped through Nimes to see the Roman arena. Girl Scouts were rendezvousing therein for some kind of encampment. We didn't disturb Lawrence Durrell at his nearby country home. Writers should be left to write. On we sped, destination Montpellier, university town where Rabelais gained his M.D. in the year 1530. A Sunday fair was in progress in the central square. We checked in at the hotel, then explored the fair, full of giddy, gaudy, noisy concessions, and enchanted children.

On south in the morning through the muscatel town of Frontignan, stashing a couple of golden bottles in the bonnet, traversing the island town of Sète, made famous by Valéry's *Cimitière Marin*, taking coffee break in Perpignan, near Maillol's home village and also the Casals' festival town of Prades; finally passing through the lowest part of the easternmost Pyrenees, by an oak-forested creek-valley, the snowy mountains to the west; and across the frontier at Jonquera, a village jammed with fruit and vegetable trucks bound for the French markets.

Spain at last, after a lifetime of reading; rivers with scant flow, belled sheep and goats and cows, women and men toiling by hand, a poor, self-tortured land, haunted by Don Quixote and Sancho Panza, by Goya and Lorca. At Gerona we angled out to the Costa Brava for the short stretch of spectacular cliff road, passing through a cork oak forest, blessedly away from the trucking that makes Spain's main roads hazardous.

The memorable thing about the Costa Brava from San Feliu de Guixols to Tossa de Mar was not the sea road, a little Big Sur, but the mountainside of lavender and rosemary in flower, the color and the fragrance in the windy sea air.

Barcelona over night and our first 10 P.M. dinner, then on in the morning toward Valencia, passing over a stretch of coast road labeled on the map as "carretera peligrosa—route dangereuse." Indeed it was, a veritable roller coaster in and out of a hundred *barrancas* where the rocky mountainside plunged to the sea, thinly forested with olive and carob. Two newly overturned trucks confirmed the map's warning.

Then we crossed the estuary of the Ebro, a river we were to regain a week later at Zaragoza. Finally we reached the subtropical verdure of the Valencia plain and entered green gold groves of oranges in flower and fruit; and at dinner that night our waiter demonstrated his virtuosity by paring an orange in one unbroken ribbon of peel, the fruit impaled on a dagger and peeled by the knife in his other hand.

That was a meal to remember. It began with a plate of artichoke hearts with bits of ham. Poached turbot and boiled potatoes came next followed by salad, the orange, coffee. And a stroll through the animated streets before bed.

The road to Madrid leaves the citrus plain, rises through oak-forested highlands to the red-earthed mesas of Castile, crosses occasional rivers, vast grain fields, and has few travelers. At a crossing of the Rio Cabriel we switchbacked down through an elfin forest of rosemary chaparral, seeing many sheep and hearing the tintinnabulation of their bells; and then at the river we saw a dam being built with cement made on the spot with power generated by the diverted water.

Approaching Madrid and a crossing of the Rio Tejo, the Tagus, the Iberian Peninsula's greatest river, we passed through a series of rain showers. The wet red earth, the occasional dark trees and far vistas formed a landscape reminiscent of New Mexico. In Spain every branch and twig from the pruning of olives and other trees is gathered by peasants and brought to the villages on burros or *carretas* and there stacked for fuel. We saw reforestation projects being carried out with conifers on eroded slopes; and on the outskirts of the cities roads were being widened by the sacrifice of ancient plane trees. Another sign of spring was the manuring of the soil, as the winter droppings were brought out from barns, dumped in piles, and spread by hand, usually by women.

We did not stay long enough to get much feeling for Madrid. Big cities take time. Each day we walked a couple of miles down the Paseo from our hotel in the Avenida General Sanjurjo to the center, calling for mail at Amexco, then for café con leche in a circular café, shopping for gifts and a book or two. The Prado was the high point, and in it the huge painting by Hieronymus Bosch of "The Garden of Delights," in which Surrealism begins and ends.

On Good Friday we took a bus tour to Toledo. It rained. The cathedral was crowded with worshippers, tourists, and just plain people trying to keep dry. It was like the May Company basement on Dollar Day. There was a stench of wet woolens. A roomful of Grecos was obliterated by a single Goya in their midst, a glowing picture of Christ taken Prisoner, possessed of that heartbreaking quality which makes Goya and Rembrandt blood brothers.

Trying to find our way back to the bus we got lost in the mazy streets, packed with promenaders in spite of the rain. In desperation we took a cab to the Hotel Monterrey where we rejoined our party for lunch. Too many to be served well. The *paella* was poor. Then a final view of the city from across the Tagus at the point where El Greco painted Toledo rising like flames into the sky.

Gradually it comes over you in Spain that the country and the people are like no others. What is it about the Spaniards that differentiates them from their neighbors? Pride, cynicism, irony, mordant humor are some of the qualities, apparent even in the garage attendants who serviced the car, six of them doing what two Frenchmen had done, one Swiss. When I came to watch, they stopped and began to joke and laugh at me and the car, though not in a mean way; so I laughed too, at God knows what.

Madrid to Zaragoza again was pure New Mexico, the road following dry river courses burning with peach and cherry trees in bloom, occasional villages of colored adobe, and slopes which sheep had threaded with trails, and few people. High above one such arroyo we spied what looked like a Roman arch, silhouetted against the sky. Our Michelin map confirmed it. *Arca romana*. We branched off on a road which led to it, parked nearby, and picnicked to the sound of sheep bells, the omnipresent Spanish leitmotiv. I understood for the first time why the conquistadors and missionaries of the sixteenth and seventeenth centuries felt so much at home in New Mexico, as they ascended the Rio Grande from El Paso to Taos.

It was late afternoon when we crossed the last rocky range and looked down on the plain of Zaragoza, the sunlit city framed in green fields and groves, which in turn were hemmed by golden grain.

This fair vision yielded to the reality of a long search for our hotel, the Goya; finally found by trial and error among the short narrow streets of town center. It was the poorest hotel of our trip. Our room was located on the top floor, beneath the elevator machinery. A pitiful terrace yielded a view over bare rooftops. I was fighting a cold. We were too tired to stay up for the customary late dinner, and then our sleep was interrupted toward midnight by retiring guests congregated in the halls outside our room and talking loudly. Finally I got up and pounded on the door. Silence. Scattering footsteps. The sound of room doors being closed. They must have thought my knocking was a signal by Franco's eavesdropping secret police.

On leaving Zaragoza in the morning we stopped at the cathedral and in spite of the early hour found it full of worshippers, come to one of Spain's great shrines—the Little Virgin of El Pilar—a doll almost lost in the ornate baroque setting in which she stood. (We were glad later that we had paid this visit to her shrine.) The cathedral was heated by grilled floor furnaces, the smoke from which had ruined the frescoes on which Goya had worked. We made one drifting round, then left.

We crossed the Ebro on a beautiful old stone bridge, lingered on the far side, and looked back on the towers and trees of Zaragoza. A great day lay ahead, the finest day of the entire trip, our crossing of the Pyrenees over the Pass of Somport, a route taken on a gamble that a spell of fair weather would controvert the guidebook which listed the Somport as one of the passes closed by snow until late in May. The day was April 15. Time pressed. We were heading for Pau, Toulouse, Albi, and a rendezvous with Georges Connes near the gorges of the River Tarn, and I did not want to detour around either of the low passes at the Mediterranean and Atlantic ends of the Pyrenees.

Where the road continued toward Barcelona we turned north to Huesca. Though the day was clear no sight was had of the mountains we knew were there. The only evidence that they *were* there was in the sky—a faint line of cumulus clouds on the horizon; and as we climbed slowly over the rising plain of Aragon at last the Pyrenees began to appear. Foothills first, then blue shoulders, and finally the white peaks, hard to distinguish from the clouds.

At Huesca we turned west and entered a long lonely stretch of road. I was alert for approaching traffic with French or other foreign license plates, which would mean that the Somport Pass was open. None. Nor any going our way. No one. At a crossing of the Rio Gallego, running wild with white water, we stopped to watch a flock of sheep stream down the hillside, cross the bridge, and flow up the other side, accompanied by one shepherd and two working dogs. No words were spoken by the cloaked man, no barking of his dogs; all went beautifully forward with only the sound of bells. When the last of the sheep were lost from sight, though not sound, we set out again on our lonely way. The omens were ominous.

The road began to rise through foothills up the pass of Santa Barbara, leading to the valley of the Rio Aragon, and it was still a deserted way. What had happened to the world? I tasted fear on my tongue. And then, we reached the summit; and there before us, beyond the river valley was a breathtaking sight of the Pyrenees, a long white line of battlements haunted by the ghost of Roland. What other mountain range of the world has such a guardian hero?

Now we dropped fast to the crossroads of decision. Westward, downriver, the road led to Pamplona, San Sebastian, St. Jean de Luz, Biarritz, and the low Atlantic way around the mountains. Eastward, upriver, to Jaca where the Aragon turned north and entered the range, the pass road followed the narrowing canyon on up and over and into France.

Was the Somport open? At the crossroads an innkeeper thought that it was, although southbound traffic failed to prove it. It was a tidy new inn and we ate lunch at an outdoor table in the courtyard— potato omelette, bread, grapes, and coffee.

Courage and resolution came with the food. We took the eastward road following the Aragon, running high and white with snow melt; and having stopped at Jaca for gasoline, we met a French truck, freshly through the pass from Oloron, hauling a load of farm machinery to Huesca. "Barely open," the driver said; "plowed though this morning. But hurry," he urged, "snow is forecast."

Seen from the summit of the Pass of Santa Barbara, the Pyrenees presented an unbroken wall, but as we came closer canyons appeared, culs-de-sac all but one, with roads dead-ending at ancient hamlets, such as Hecho and Anso where, the innkeeper told us, life is unchanged from the Middle Ages.

At last the Aragon turned and entered the mountains by a narrow, winding, steep canyon, up which the Porsche climbed like a good

Spanish burro, sure-wheeled and responsive, on up the rocky gorge, with pine trees and snow peaks and waterfalls on either side, the blue sky overhead. And, incredibly, a railroad track, on the opposite side of the gorge, and even more unbelievable, a little train, toiling upward, drawn by two stubby engines, belching coal smoke, and stoked by wild-looking, gesticulating firemen. Its coaches were crowded with passengers at the windows; and as we overtook the train and pulled ahead, they shouted and waved, the firemen shoveled, the engineers shrilled their whistles, and I honked. We came into the station of Canfranc a minute ahead of the train. The passengers poured out, and we saw that they were mostly skiers, who shouldered their equipment and headed for the high white slopes. A group of them admired the Porsche. It was the only one we saw in all of Spain.

Here we went through immigration and customs formalities, seeing Spanish officials wearing uniforms of the Napoleonic era and moving with the deliberateness of entrenched bureaucrats. The frontier itself was a mile beyond, just short of the summit; and as we approached a barrier across the road, a sentry came out of a hut, singing to himself, glanced at our papers, raised the barrier, and we were in France. As we neared the actual crest on the narrow road plowed deep through snowbanks, I pulled up short with relief to get out and wet my dry mouth with snow—just as a rock slide came roaring down and across the road ahead; a dozen massive boulders, loosened by the thaw, went bounding down the gorge. It was then that we gave thanks to El Pilar.

Over the summit the road dropped swiftly down the Gave d'Aspe into a green river valley as prosperous, civilized, and secure as the Spanish side was not. The French control point was comfortably below the snow line. Cattle, sheep, farms, trees in full leaf—a fertility the result of the way the mountains milk the Atlantic storm clouds of their rain and leave none for Spain. Through the foothills of the French side, the region of Béarn, we descended to Oloron and then to Pau, where we came at the end of that long dramatic day, relieved to find a good lodging in a hotel on the Boulevard des Pyrenees, our room looking out on the green and blue jumble of foothills and the great white wall beyond. We had made it!

We liked peaceful, provincial Pau from a stroll around town center and a good dinner on the main square, cooked by the woman proprietor and served by a deft young waiter. We left secure in that atmosphere of small restaurants no matter where in France, with their religious concern for the preparation, serving, and eating of food, the stuff and the staff of life, rites that are central in French culture.

We drove eastward in the morning, along the edge of the foothills, scattered with flowering wild trees and backed by the endless white range, came later on the Garonne, chief river of southwestern France, and followed it toward Toulouse. At noon we stopped in the village of St. Martory at the Hotel de France, recommended by Michelin. Its façade was drab, its courtyard dirty, but as soon as we entered the dining room, tabled with fat people deep in their meal, and saw displays of faience and flowers and smelled good things cooking, we knew that Michelin had not erred. The meal was memorable: hors d'oeuvre including bits of tender beef (yesterday's leftover entrée), *omelette jambon*, endive salad, and infused coffee.

By the time we reached Toulouse cold rain was falling. The Somport Pass would be closed by snow. By the grace of God we had come through on the one day it was open. Beyond Toulouse we reached the Tarn and followed the wide green river to Albi. Again we proposed a predinner stroll, but the rain drove us into the Grand Café on the Place Wigan and there we dried out over coffee, read the *Dépêche de Toulouse*, and watched and heard fat men at cards and conversation, also part of the blessed ambiance of the French café.

By morning the rain had stopped. We walked to the red brick cathedral, toured the cold interior where I wanted particularly to see the provocative sculpture of Judith, described in Freda White's *Three Rivers of France*; and then to the adjoining Musée Lautrec, where in

his natal town the crippled artist's greatest legacy is hung. The Cha-
teau Museum overlooks the Tarn, weir-wide at this point. Few people
were in the unheated museum. We hurried through, our heels click-
ing on the parquet floors.

We took the road on upriver to lunch at Requista and our rendezvous at Villefranche de Panat with my old Dijon professor, Georges
Connes. That village is not on most maps. At the auto club in Nice
they couldn't find it at all. The girl confidently assured me that "ça
n'existe pas." So I had written ahead to Connes and he had replied to
Madrid, with a hand-drawn map which located the hamlet.

As we switchbacked down through the leafless chestnut forest, we
saw him waiting at the bridge over a creek. "Vers trois heures," we
had set the rendezvous. It was five after three. "Good staff work," he
cried, sweeping us into a bear hug. I had tears in my eyes at this re-
union with one of the three great teachers I have known.

So remote is Connes' ancestral farm (his family has been there
since 1404) in the mountainous Rouergue above the river village of
Le Truel, that he had to lead us in his Citroën 2-CV over the last few
miles to the point where we parked the Porsche in his neighbor's
piggery, transferred to his car, and crawled the final quarter-mile
down a muddy wagon track to where his old stone house stood on a
ledge, a thousand feet above the Tarn, in the midst of the chestnut
forest that dominates the region.

Connes had just arrived from Dijon on his first visit since October
and found that the coldest winter in a century had left his water pipes
frozen. The electricity was off. The olive oil was unpourable. Rain
was falling. We all knew what to do. I carried water from a pump,
then logs, while my wife made the beds, and our host cooked an
omelette and set the table with bread and butter and wine. We ate by
firelight, then talked for hours to the sound of rain on the roof and a
deep distant hum.

A clearing morning disclosed what that sound was: we were di-
rectly above one of the power stations at a dam on the Tarn. Elec-

tricité de France has developed this stretch of the river in the manner of our Tennessee Valley Authority.

Later we made a three-hour, fifty-mile reconnaissance of the region in the Citroën, snailing down to the river, over, and up the other side, visiting nooks and crannies where the peasants live a life changed only by electricity. Life is hard there in the Rouergue and the young people are leaving the land for the cities. An old story.

In the village of Saint-Victor, population 100, whose economy is providing ewes' milk to nearby Roquefort, the restored church contains recent frescoes by Nicolas Greschny, a wandering Estonian painter. We surmounted manure piles, entered, and were dazzled by the ardent depiction of biblical scenes and personages, painted in primary colors, using local models and including the painter's self-portrait. The inscriptions throughout were lettered in both Latin and Langue d'Oc.

Georges Connes is known throughout the region for the heroic role he played in the Occupation and Liberation, and when, upon retirement from the university and after he had served as postwar mayor of Dijon, he came back to the mountains of his ancestors, the locals wanted him to be mayor of Le Truel. "My friends," he said, "governing 100,000 was easy; to govern 560 quite another matter. Let us remain friends. My answer is *no*."

After two days of such memorable primitive existence we left him going in search of a plumber and headed north to Rodez, county seat of the Aveyron, then on across the River Lot and onto the plateau of the Haute Auvergne, the volcanic backbone of France known as Le Massif Central, following a bleak, snow-edged road, spring lost again, white peaks to the east and to the west, through high sheep country, the walls, houses, barns all built of the gray rock, lonely, austere, forbidding. I kept hearing Jennie Tourel's singing of the "Shepherd's Song of the Auvergne," and wishing for a copy of *Travels with a Donkey*, R.L.S.'s essays about the Cevennes to the east of us.

We had planned to cross the mountains to the Dordogne and visit the caves of Lascaux, but from a chance reading of Connes' copy of *Figaro Littéraire* we learned that organisms on the rock walls were threatening to obliterate the frescoes and the caves had been closed to tourists. So we kept due north, lunched at St. Fleur, stone-gray county seat of the Cantal where market day jammed the streets and square.

Later in a village we were slowed to a halt by a cattle fair which blocked the street. The owners looked as primitive as their beasts.

On we pressed to Clermont-Ferrand, the industrialized ugly city center of the region, then desended to a more fertile land, the Charolle, where the snow-white Charolais cattle, France's finest beef, made pastoral pictures in fields of bright green.

Vichy for the night, ours to choose among a hundred empty preseason hotels. Here my congested liver finally rebelled and I stayed in bed for two days, barely able to tolerate grapefruit juice and water, Vichy of course.

Our next stop was Vézelay, the hill village from whose Romanesque Basilique de la Madeleine the Dijonnais St. Bernard preached the Second and Third Crusades, and to which thirty years before in my Burgundian life I used to bicycle for halcyon weekends. At the Hotel de la Poste et du Lion d'Or, thickly starred in Michelin, I had to forego the rich cuisine and let my wife eat alone, a delicious, ritualistic dinner with local Chablis to drink, she reported later when she returned to our room. I groaned.

In the morning we toiled up the steep street that spined the hill to the basilica, its cream and rose limestone nave free of the usual clutter of cathedral statuary, its capitals grotesquely carved, then walked on the esplanade under the newly leafed chestnut trees, overlooking the idyllic valley of the Cure. I was recuperating and longed to linger there between Burgundy and the Morvan as the month of May was about to explode in flower, but cities and people and duty called. In Paris and London were friends to see, books to buy, speeches to make. Our freedom had come to an end.

South from Lisbon

T H E approach of winter on a day when London's cold penetrated my several layers of wool sent me running to the office of Portuguese Airways in Lower Regent Street.

"I want a ticket to Lisbon," I said to the olive-skinned girl at the counter.

"Ah," she said, "It *is* the time to go south." She drew a shawl closer around her shoulders. "I wish I were going."

"Do you live in Lisbon?"

"Coimbra," she said, "the university town north of Lisbon. You will go there, yes?"

"I go south from Lisbon."

"South? There is nothing south of Lisbon."

"Oh yes there is. There is Cape St. Vincent."

"I have never been there," she admitted, "but I believe that it is a barren headland. Perhaps a lighthouse. Nothing more."

"There is more," I said. "There is poetry and history."

"Are you a poet? You don't look like one."

"I am a ghost-hunter. I go to Cape St. Vincent to look for ghosts."

I saw that she wanted an explanation, but other customers had come in, and I fell silent while she wrote out my ticket.

Wind and rain marked departure the next day from London Airport. The TAP Caravelle climbed sharply through the cloud cover and flew above it all the way to Portugal, then slipped through a rift in the white mass to land neatly at Lisbon Airport.

I was in Portugal, fabled Lusitania, a fulfillment of years of desire, composed of various elements. The maritime discoverer of California was a Portuguese—João Rodrigues Cabrilho. He had probably learned navigation in the celebrated school at Sagres, in the lee of Cape St. Vincent, founded by Prince Henry the Navigator, then had sailed for Spain as Juan Rodriguez Cabrillo.

That was the historical lure of the Cape. The poetical came from Browning, his "Home Thoughts from the Sea," and its opening line, "Nobly, nobly Cape St. Vincent to the Northwest died away," and from Fernando Pessoa, the shadowy Lisbon poet, who wrote under various names in several languages, including English. I cherish a copy of his *English Poems*, given to me long ago by Richard Aldington, with its sensuous "Epithalamium," one of the most beautiful wedding poems in our language.

Lisbon was one of the few European capitals I had never seen. It is like no other. I spent my first week there in mild weather, becoming accustomed to the speech, the rhythm, and the ambiance of a new way of life, finding the Portuguese people cordial and honest. Overpayment to such varied personages as a taxi driver, a waiter in the Hotel Ritz, and a street peddler of bananas, resulted each time in the mistake being pointed out and the coins returned to me.

I brought with me no judgment of the Salazar regime. Personal indignation felt by a foreigner over another country's social and economic system seems to me a waste of emotion. As a student in France a generation earlier, I was naturally involved in various social judgments. Coming now to Portugal as a middle-aged traveler, I felt free to look and listen, to use my senses and my wits to guide me each day as I walked and rode about Lisbon, admiring the public monuments to men of arts and letters as well as to military and political figures. The sidewalks are paved in mosaic patterns of colored limestone pebbles. Streets are cobbled. Taxis are a uniform fleet of Mercedes 180 Diesels. Their characteristic knock is Lisbon's leitmotiv.

Lisbon is hills and harbor, served by a wide central boulevard with swan pools and papyrus, off which run narrow curving streets and alleys, all dropping eventually to the waterfront, to Lisbon's noble harbor, the wide estuary of the Tagus, ocean's end of the river I had seen last three years before in Spain, where it all but enisles Toledo.

I watched a string of barges arrive from upriver and tie up at a dock. They were full of yellow wheat. A team of dockers with shovels began to sack the grain, then carry the heavy sacks on their shoulders to a scale where a weighmaster entered each one in an open ledger. Then the sacks were loaded into little freight cars. Automation has not reached the Lisbon waterfront.

Farther along the embankment is the monastery church with the tombs of Camões and Vasco da Gama; the museum of coaches, an assemblage of eighteenth-century vehicles gorgeously gilded and painted; and nearby, the colossal monument to Prince Henry the Navigator and his followers, a huge work of concrete and stone sculpture erected in 1960 on the 500th anniversary of the Navigator's death.

Near this harbor point is the new bridge over the Tagus, Europe's longest suspension bridge. Until it opened in August, 1966, bridging the estuary for the first time, the only way across to the south had been by auto ferry or a three-hour drive upriver to the first bridge.

"Heading south?" they asked as incredulously as the girl in London, when I hired a Volkswagen 1500 and inquired the way from city center to the Tagus bridge. "Tourists always head north."

"My destination is Lagos, Sagres, and Cape St. Vincent," I insisted. "Not Estoril, Coimbra, or Oporto."

"But there's nothing down there. No cultural centers. Only sand, sheep, and sardines."

"And the Prince's ghost," I said, heading south from Lisbon.

The road follows the ridges and valleys of the first range of hills from the Atlantic shore, through forests of eucalyptus and cork oak, the ocean far below on the right and in the east the distant blue sierra between Portugal and Spain. Traffic was light. There are few towns and villages. The flora changes to olive, fig, and almond, orange, and lemon. Sandy earth turns red. Whitewashed, flat-topped farm houses, trimmed in blue, show the Moorish influence. The peasants' carts bear colorful decorations. This is the province of Algarve, from the Moorish, meaning the West.

The Atlantic is reached at Lagos (lagoon), and there on the waterfront is another monument to Prince Henry, depicting the seated Navigator looking over the harbor where his caravels once anchored. It too was dedicated on the anniversary in 1960. A wide sandy beach curves east from Lagos eight miles to Portomaio, a strand strewn with clam and scallop shells—and no people. Here and there sardine boats are beached. They too are brightly decorated. My hotel was the Meia Praia—the Middle Beach—and in early December there were more employees than guests. Meals were served with courteous elegance. The seafood was varied and cooked within hours of catching. Royalty could not have fared better.

Eastward forty miles to Faro, the capital, the coast of Algarve becomes rockier. The most fashionable resort is Praia da Rocha, but even it has none of the *luxe* that marks the French Riviera. It is still a comparatively unspoiled coast. Back from the beaches the land rises to hills and low mountains, the Sierra Monchique. Fig, citrus, and almond orchards yield to carob groves and then cork oak. The heavy red soil is fertile. Most of the farming is still done with primitive equipment.

Time has lightly touched this sheltered coast. The Moors have long since been driven back across the Atlantic to Africa. Their ancient stronghold of Silves is on a hill a few miles from the shore. It looks like a cubist painter's dream of a city, geometrically formed and planed, all dazzling white with blue and pink tile roofs and a great fortress with an underground reservoir to hold a year's water in case of siege.

I explored no further than Silves, pausing there to look back over the cultivated coast to the rocky beaches and the fishing harbor at Portomaio and the long sandy *praia* sweeping west to Lagos. I cast a longing eye inland and higher to the sierra, where the best recent book on Algarve, by David Wright and Patrick Swift, describes remote villages of unchanged customs and almost tropical verdure.

My compass pointed west, magnetized by the cape I had come to see. I drove there on a cool day of the prevailing northerly. My goal lay about fifteen miles from Lagos through more of the rich red soil planted mostly to figs. The old trees were winter bare, their silvery limbs like sprawling spiders. The approach to the cape is by the small town of Sagres. It was there that Prince Henry's monastic school was located.

The cape is a couple of miles northward across a small bay. It is a rocky headland, the basalt cliffs rising sheer two hundred feet from the ocean. There is deep water everywhere, and shipping comes in close as it turns the corner to and from the Mediterranean. *Aqui é o fim do mundo*, the Portuguese declare. Here is the end of the world. The ancient appellation of Cape St. Vincent was Promontorium Sacrum, the Sacred Cape, from which Sagres derives its name. Here at the final limit of the world, the gods were supposed to rest at night after the labors of the day. The cape owes its present name to the legend that it was here that the corpse of St. Vincent, an Iberian martyr who died in 304, was washed up by the sea.

And here is Europe's farthest southwest. It is where the Navigator lived for the last forty years of his life and trained his sailors in that art of navigation which led, after his death, to the discovery and development of the whole wide world. Vasco da Gama, Cabral, Magellan, and Columbus, that Italian married to a Portuguese and sailing for Spain—these and others owed their discoveries and fame to the sciences correlated and taught in the Prince's cosmopolitan school.

Cabrillo either studied at Sagres a generation after Henry's death, or was taught by someone who had; and so there is that link between Cape St. Vincent and California, discovered by Cabrillo in 1542. Little is known of him, other than what is in the log of his voyage, and his death in 1543 and probable burial on the island of San Miguel off the coast at Santa Barbara.

I stood in the wind on the prow of the headland, trying to remember all of Browning's lines. The only building is the lighthouse. A flock of brown and black goats browsed to the edge, some even surefooting over in search of the tiny foliage in the crevices. The long Atlantic swell rose and fell on the cape's ankle. I counted eight ships turning the southwest corner. Those heading north plunged their bows deep in the swell, lifted, plunged, lifted, all in a slow rhythm with the elements. Seabirds screamed overhead. I felt nostalgia for the sea voyages of my youth, and sensed many ghostly presences, all friendly. Mission accomplished, I turned away.

Back in Lisbon I continued to ignore the cultural north and went instead even farther south than Algarve. On a mild and rainy afternoon I took a TAP Constellation flight to Funchal, capital of Madeira, the volcanic island off the coast of Spanish Morocco. It was discovered in 1418 by a caravel expedition sent out from Lagos by Prince Henry. Now it came on the horizon as cumulus clouds over the peaks, then red rock steeps, heavily wooded (Madeira means wood), and on the westward side intricately terraced and farmed. The airstrip is a new one, carved out of a ledge near the sea, and the approach is over deep blue water. Funchal is fifteen miles distant by taxi along a narrow cliff road, snaking in and out of canyons which indent the plunging mountainside. The vegetation is dense and colorful—hibiscus, bougainvillea, geranium, bananas. Every tiny farm has a miniature plantation. Portugal's bananas all come from Madeira. The trellised vines that produce the celebrated wine were bare, and carrots and potatoes were being raised beneath the arbors.

Funchal is built in a great natural amphitheater rising from harbor to peak, a conglomeration of colored stuccos and greenery. The earliest settlers from Portugal fired the woods to make a clearing. The resulting conflagration raged over the island for seven years. The volcanic soil thus enriched by ashes is responsible for the present riot of vegetation.

I stayed in the Savoy Hotel, built in 1900 and still offering amenities of the Victorian age. The dining room is of great beauty, paneled in white and green and gold, with a mezzanine all the way

around. Multi-course meals were served formally, each table having
a carrying waiter and a serving waiter. I counted thirty-five guests
and twenty-two waiters. Again the seafood was of delicious variety
and freshness. The chef has been at the Savoy for forty-five years, I
was told, and is aided by twenty sub-chefs. An orchestra plays for
concert and dancing.

The Portuguese of Madeira are as courteous and honest as their
kinfolk at home. Tourism has miraculously left them unspoiled. After a sightseeing tour I settled into a quiet routine, the high point of
which was the afternoon walk to the harbor to see what ships were
in. Funchal is a port of call for the Union Castle Line between England and South Africa and for Portuguese liners between Lisbon and
Brazil. They stop only for a few hours. Passengers go ashore and buy
lace, basketry, wine, and bananas. A ship from Rio was passengered
with every shade of colored folk, lively and laughing. An English
motor yacht was in, taking the long way back from Gibraltar to
Southampton. The deck officer allowed the crew was homesick, hoping the owner would change her plan to stay in Funchal for the New
Year's Eve fireworks.

A friend at home had charged me to search the English Cemetery
for the grave of Emily Shore, one of the many English consumptives
who died in Madeira during the first half of the nineteenth century.
Her diary was published fifty years after her death in 1842. My
friend had read it and wondered if her grave could be found.

First I had to find the cemetery. Up the hill from the harbor, was
the general direction given me. And so up the hill I trudged along a
curving, cobbled street, dwellings and garden walls on each side of
such height as to prevent me from taking bearings. Then I saw a clue:
several tall Italian cypresses. I threaded and climbed until I came to
the high wall behind which the trees were growing. And a locked gate.
It was the cemetery. I pulled the bell cord and waited a long while.
Finally a young man came, bowed, smiled, and let me in.

I spent an hour in a vain search for Emily Shore's grave. In addition to the cypresses, an ancient pepper tree dominated the graveyard. Shrubs and vines grew in such profusion as to obscure many of the stones and markers. On some the lettering was obliterated. Emily's was probably one of those. I gave up the search and made my way back down hill to the main square. There at a sidewalk café I looked out on the statue of Madeira's discoverer, João Gonsalves Zarco, dispatched from Lagos by Prince Henry to cruise the African coast. In Funchal the Prince takes second place to the island's discoverer—a smaller square, a smaller statue.

The oxen-drawn tourist sleds slid by on the smooth cobbles. Flower and lace peddlers drifted past in courteous solicitation. An urchin shined my shoes for pennies. I studied the shipping news in the weekly paper, as showers of soft rain alternated with sunbursts. Then I saw a double rainbow arching over Funchal.

That good omen heralded my departure on the return flight to Lisbon. I gambled on a punctual arrival, for I had only a forty-five-minute interval before a Swissair flight from Zurich and Geneva left for New York. As we landed, I saw the DC-8 taxiing in, a minute ahead of us. I relaxed.

As the great white plane with the Helvetian cross on its tail soared up over the Tagus estuary, my last sight of Lisbon was of the monument to the Navigator and his men and of the noble bridge which had led me to Algarve and the Cape. Then swiftly we were over the Atlantic, westbound for America, my ultimate destination that of Cabrillo, the seacoast of California. *Aqui é o fim do mundo.*

Remembering Henry Miller

T HE death of Henry Miller six months short of his eighty-ninth
birthday has led me to look back at our friendship which began
in the winter of 1931-32 when we met in passing on the staircase of the
Faculty of Letters at the University of Dijon. I was a graduate student, writing my thesis on the poetry of Robinson Jeffers and finding
that the California settings appeared tiny and cameo-clear when seen
from afar, as it were, through the wrong end of the telescope. Miller
came to Dijon as a *répétiteur d'anglais* in the Lycée Carnot. His supervisor was Jean Matruchot, a stocky Burgundian who had served as an
interpreter with the Franco-American forces at Dijon during World
War I.

Matruchot and I had met soon after my arrival in September, 1930.
I wore a beard then, and when he first saw me he was startled; for,
he said later, I was the living image of his young brother, a sculptor
apprenticed to Rodin, who had been killed on the last day of the war.
We became friends. As Miller and I were the only American bache-
lors in town, Matruchot thought we would enjoy meeting.

It didn't work out that way. Miller felt himself in exile from Paris
and Anaïs Nin, while I was spending my time on a study of the California poet. Hanging over my head was the public defense of my thesis, and although it was not scheduled to take place until later that
year, I was dreading the ordeal. We didn't meet again, and Miller
soon went back to Paris.

Back in Los Angeles in 1934 I went to work for Jake Zeitlin, the
antiquarian bookseller. Notices came from a Paris publisher herald-
ing *Tropic of Cancer*, a novel by Henry Miller. Later I received a copy
from Monsieur Matruchot, and with it an angry letter denouncing
Miller as a wastrel. I did not understand what he meant until I read

the book with its diatribe against Lycée Carnot. Unlike my fruitful Dijon residence, Miller's had been bitterly disappointing. Although his book moved me deeply I did not try to convince the outraged Matruchot that here was a new work of genius.

By 1941 I was a junior member of the University of California at Los Angeles library staff, sustained by an inner conviction (shared by no one else) that if I worked hard and was patient and had a bit of luck, I would eventually head that library. Then one day in the spring of that year there stood Henry Miller at my desk. When he embarked on the cross-country trip that resulted in *The Air-Conditioned Nightmare*, his publisher James Laughlin had urged him to look up Larry Powell, a librarian already notorious for reading books and whose library had been the first to place a standing order for New Directions publications. I was not surprised by his arrival, for Miller had sent me a reprint from the *Criterion* of his essay on Anaïs Nin, "Un Etre Etoilique," with the inscription "For Larry Powell, hoping to see you soon. Henry Miller. 11/26/40."

It was the afternoon of May 25, 1941, when Miller found me typing up faculty book orders. In recalling our previous meeting, we agreed that it *had* been a mighty cold winter. After charging out a book that he had been seeking all the way across the country (it was Jacob Boehme's *Aurora, or The Morning Rednesse*, a title Yeats thought the loveliest ever given a book), we made a date for him to dine at our home.

My wife and I and our two small sons lived in Beverly Glen, a canyon in the Santa Monica mountains north of the UCLA campus. Our home was a glorified cabin. After dinner two days later Miller inscribed the copy of his book sent me by Jean Matruchot: "For Larry Powell whom I am delighted to meet again here in California after the romantic days in Dijon when Matruchot taught the poor little buggers 'John Gilpin's Ride'—why, I don't know. Faithfully yours, Henry Miller, 5/27/41." His memories of Lycée Carnot had mellowed!

Miller liked the canyon setting with its proximity to Hollywood, about which he had dreams of getting rich as a script writer. His letters to Anaïs Nin published in 1965 and her diaries of that period tell of his unsuccessful efforts. During the next two years Miller headquartered in Beverly Glen where he lived with Gilbert and Margaret Neiman, a talented bilingual couple who had been in Mexico.

Life was simple in those early years of the war. Gas rationing kept us close to home. Those of us young fathers who were temporarily exempt from the draft felt twinges of guilt. I applied for a job as a Greyhound bus driver, although I ended as a laborer in a war plant making arctic sleeping bags and kapok life jackets for the armed forces —a scenario right out of Kafka.

Evenings were enlivened by potluck suppers with other young couples who lived in Beverly Glen. None of us had much money. In 1941 my library salary was $1,740 a year. Miller's meager income was from uncertain sources. It was not until after the war when he was able to draw on French royalties and in the 1960s when the courts cleared his *Tropic of Cancer* and *Tropic of Capricorn* for American publication that Miller became affluent. To the end of his life he was prodigally generous with whatever he had, however little.

In Beverly Glen, Miller sold his deliberately childlike watercolors for anything offered, fifty cents or a dollar. One night he brought an armful as a supper offering. Afterward, a bit high on Escondido muscatel, he seized the paintings and threw them on the fire as unworthy of Fay's dinner of meat loaf, romaine, French bread, Monterey jack cheese, fruit, and coffee. She managed to save one from burning—a bold self-portrait. She still has it.

Miller was given to sudden theatrical acts, such as the time when with our youngest son, age six, we stopped by Miller's cabin down Glen to leave some books from the library. When the child coveted pennies on the table, Miller emptied his pocket of change and thrust it on the boy. I let him keep only the pennies, knowing that Henry probably didn't have any more than he'd fished from his pocket.

After he had sold his Buick for $75 and his books for much less, Miller had to thumb his way out of the canyon to Sunset Boulevard.

Sometimes he borrowed fifty cents from us for the bus trip to Hollywood and back, never failing to repay it. That was the time of his
letter in the *New Republic*, asking for old clothes. When a tuxedo arrived, he made a scarecrow and hung it on the front fence throughout the rainy winter.

By February, 1944, when Miller left Beverly Glen for Big Sur,
where he lived for the next fifteen years, our friendship had reached
the point where each had something the other needed. After I had
rather miraculously become head librarian of UCLA, I shamelessly
used my position to serve Miller's needs, providing a repository for
his manuscripts and rising flood of fan mail, as well as mailing him a
constant supply of books. This resulted eventually in *The Books in My
Life*, an account of his lifelong reading which I proposed that he
write and which he generously dedicated to me.

A more unusual service was my recommending a translator for his
newly published *The Colossus of Maroussi*. She was a Greek girl working in the library. What happened was combustion, not translation.
When Miller stopped writing poetry to the girl, he found a more
prosaic relationship with her mother. We lost a typist.

Miller had given the library his letters from Lawrence Durrell,
and on visits to Big Sur we talked of a volume of their correspondence. I was supposed to edit it. Alas, I lacked the time. Later I
found the perfect editor in Professor George Wickes. His edition of
A Private Correspondence was published in 1962.

Wickes seemed also the ideal editor of Miller's letters to the
painter Emil Schnellock. Unfortunately Miller fell out with Wickes,
a Belgian-American, and for no other apparent reason than Wickes'
spoken French. Inasmuch as the "Boy from Brooklyn's" own French
accent was so bad, though fluent, I felt that Henry was being unfair to
George. When toward the end of Miller's life I recommended Jay
Martin to write his biography, Miller grew cross with me, although
the book proved fair to Henry. He finally forgave me.

Martin's book was based on the archives at UCLA. By the time he commenced the research that took eight years to complete, the collection had grown to formidable size. Included are thousands of letters to Miller from readers of all ages and nationalities. At first he tried to answer them all, and always in the free-flowing hand that never left him even when in old age near blindness made writing difficult.

These were some of the things I did for Henry Miller. What he did for me was to recognize my creative nature that administration and other pressures threatened to bury. His response to a manuscript I had written during 1941-43 and first called "Quintet" was a long, ardent letter. Thirty-four years later it appeared as the afterword to my novella by then called *The Blue Train*. It was his affirmation, and that of a few other friends, that kept my gifts, such as they were, from being lost. I have testified at various times and places to what Miller's friendship meant to me, culminating at UCLA in January, 1972, when Lawrence Durrell came from France to join us in celebrating Miller's eightieth birthday.

Now I have been moved to search back in my journal of the Beverly Glen years for my responses to those meetings with Miller, when I was guided only by instincts for life and literature. Ever since my first reading of *Tropic of Cancer*, I continued to recognize Miller as one of our great originals, a blood brother to Walt Whitman. Our subsequent meetings confirmed my initial response, and I paid tribute to his work on every possible occasion, including a court appearance in 1962 as a witness in defense of *Tropic of Cancer*.

I saw Miller from time to time during his residence in Big Sur and then in Pacific Palisades near UCLA, where he lived until his death in 1980. When Robert Snyder was making the documentary film *The Henry Miller Odyssey*, parts were filmed in my office with Miller and me discussing his archives. As I persisted in writing romantic fiction, Miller was always encouraging.

After I had suffered several publishers' rejections, Henry bucked me up with these words: "Anyway, pay no attention to negative criticism, even if from people you believe in. Just believe in your-

self—completely. Avanti! Fuck the critics, editors and their ilk. I
do remember the warm sensuous feel of your book. You'll never
lose that. And if I may say so, don't go for perfection. Turn out one
after another—time is short. You have dozens of books in you. Bless
you, my dear Larry.''

Our last meeting was at his bedside near the end of his life when
we toasted each other in grape juice and Shasta water.

Here then is how Henry Miller appeared to me forty years ago :

May 25, 1941, Beverly Glen: Henry Miller is in town. Called me at
the Library. Brooklyn accent. Came later. Short, baldish, weak eyes,
very agreeable, slightly obsequious, perfectly integrated. Touring the
country by himself in an old car. Refused Hollywood offers. Coming
here for supper and the evening day after tomorrow. A great writer.
Presents the whole man. Terribly honest. In the tradition of Rabelais
and Whitman. I told him to go along Main and East 5th streets, to see
Los Angeles' tenderloin.

May 27, 1941: I am deeply moved by him. We had a marvelous
session. He and his books are one: a great writer and a great man.
Very kind. Liked the children. Understood them. Talks like he
writes. Becomes eloquent. Gets up and walks around the room. Acts
the characters. Talked of the Munich crisis of 1938; leaving Paris.
Being afraid. Then cleaning out everything he owned from the Villa
Seurat where he had lived for 5 or 6 years. Books, everything, liqui-
dated. Said he was becoming too attached to the place. Went to
Greece from Marseilles for a vacation. The war broke out. Sailed for
the U.S. Boat stopped day and a night in Marseilles, but he wouldn't
go ashore. Had said his farewell to France. Asked him about his early
writings in this country, from 1924 to 1927, after he quit Western
Union to be a writer. These were stories or manifestoes printed on
broadsides. About 1 a week. 20 or more. Price 10 cents. At end of
week when none had been sold, he would give them away, and when
people wouldn't take them, he would put them under doors. For 6
months he wrote a daily column for a newspaper that was never pub-

lished. The owner thought that Miller's wife was the author. Paid her $90 a week. Slept with her. Married three times. One daughter about 21. Hasn't seen her for many years. 28 years ago Miller was here in Southern California. Worked at Chula Vista near San Diego, on a lemon ranch, brush burning. Was born in 1891. A wonderfully integrated man. Won his freedom at a great price. Touring this country alone in an old Buick sedan. He wanted my Jeffers book which I was writing when we first met in Dijon 10 years ago this winter. I inscribed a copy for him. He wrote in our copies of his books. Is heading north. Back to N.Y. by the end of the year. Then to Mexico. Thence to India and China. Says he will die in about 8 or 9 years from now—a peaceful, ecstatic death. I said he would have earned it. Wants to write his Capricorn cycle. Doesn't intend to expurgate it for this country. Is indifferent to fame or publicity. Knows that he is writing an immortal work.

In our guest book that night he wrote: "May 27th 1941. Henry Miller of the 14th Ward and other places—a fine evening. Keep the aspidistra flying."

September 7, 1941: Sunday. Henry Miller dropped by this morning to say goodbye. He leaves in a day or two for S.F. and N.Y. via the northern route. Brought me two books: his own "The World of Sex"—a statement of his sexual philosophy as expressed in the two "Tropics"—an 80-page essay. Also Kenneth Patchen's "Journal of Albion Moonlight." Had lunch twice with Miller last week in the Village. He likes this region, but feels impelled to roam on. One day he wore corduroy trousers, a short-sleeved jersey, a green corduroy jacket similar to mine. On his feet leather sandals. Yesterday a nondescript gray suit. A small black-and-white checked cap. Was trying to raise money. Selling books and his own manuscripts. His car. Has been having an affair with a Mexican woman in Santa Monica. Probably why he has stayed here all summer. Also has been reading proof on his two books "Colossus of Maroussi" and "Wisdom of the Heart." I hope to write notices of both. He commented on the ease with which he can now get things published. Everyone after him for a

book. In the past he couldn't get anything published and the writing
kept pouring out of him. Now, he said, how ironical it would be if
he found that he had nothing more to say. On my looks alone, he
said, people take me for a dentist, a schoolteacher, a realtor; in fact
anything but a writer. A few hours ago he sat in this study here. Then
I saw him off down the canyon in his 1932 black Buick 4-door sedan,
with orange and black New York license plates. One of the last things
he said was that he had a hunch that I would be offered a big job in
the East. Farewell Henry!

July 22, 1942: Yesterday saw Henry Miller; he has come west
after a year in N.Y., and is living down near the mouth of the Glen.

On August 22: We had the Neimans with him to dinner. They
wrote in Spanish in our guest book. and Henry took off with this
characteristic exuberant nonsense:

> A quiver, a quaver
> A shiver, a shaver
> A sliver, a slaver
> A liver, a laver
> Lavabo!

Par ici, m'sieus dames
Je t'embrasse amicalement
Sur ta douce bouche
de la bain douche.

Un jour quand je me suis trompé, je disais à un ami
"qu'est-ce que tu a,
salaud tu es!"
Alors, l'autre, repond-t'il:
"Tu es fou? Toi?"
"Moi?"
"Toi!"

Encore une fois je t'embrasse. J'aime mieux embrasser
   toi que moi.
Moi je suis toujours un peu conasse.
Je t'embrasse.

Night of the quavering fiddle-faddle douzième siècle.

September 13, 1942: Henry Miller again. Has been here for about
two months, living down the Glen with friends. Have had several ses-
sions. Here for lunch yesterday. Drove him home and he loaded me
with manuscripts to store for him. His American book. Chaotic.
Full of magnificent passages, windy discourses, discursions. He is
abundant. Best of all a huge typescript—copies of letters he wrote to
his New York friend, Emil, from 1922 to 1939; but mostly from
Paris 1930 on. He arrived in Paris on March 4, 1930, just a few months
before I did, and for a year or more he lived a vagabond existence,
hand to mouth, exalted and miserable. He was then nearly 40 years
old, and plagued with the realization that he was completely unknown
and unaccepted as a writer. The grandeur and misery of Paris. The
exploration of the myriad streets. What a portrait of a city! A book
must be made of these letters. Miller wants it; that is why he had
them typed out, but no publisher as yet. They form one of the greatest accounts of Paris ever written. Whereas his earlier letters written
from N.Y. are arty and wordy, full of posing and rhetoric, those from
Paris are desperately sincere, lyrical, naked, magnificent. For example,
March 5, 1931: "You know I have had a pretty rich life thus far.
Well, this past year has been the epitome of all the years preceding.
I feel now as all the great vagabond artists must have felt—absolutely
reckless, childlike, irresponsible, unscrupulous, and overflowing with
carnal vitality, vigor, ginger, etc. Always on the border of insanity
due to worry, hunger, etc. But shoving along, day after day. I have
crammed so damn much in that I am on the point of snapping. If I
were told tomorrow that I must hang, I would say O.K. I've seen the

show.'' Strange the way our paths have crossed and recrossed! How thin his reactions make my own. But I was only 23 when I first saw Paris and absolutely unschooled in self-expression. On the threshold of my adult life. And by the time I last saw Paris, three years later, my capacity for experience had been greatly enlarged; and those last few days in Paris I knew some of the same exaltation H. M. felt there through the 30s. Strange too that Miller's first abode was in the Quartier St. Germain des Près; in fact he lived in the hotel St. G. at 36 rue Bonaparte, the same one Ritchie inhabited while working at Schmied's. Will I ever return to Paris? And if I do, who will I be at that epoch? What my capacity for experience? Thank God the future is unknown to us. Prescience of it would lead surely to madness. As it is, the mystery, the hope, are delicious. I should write a portrait of Miller.

Henry came for dinner on September 19, 1942, and wrote the following in our guest book:''Well, Larry me lad, here we are again. Remember that astrology did not begin in Babylonia but on the lost continent of Mu whence we derived it telaesthetically thru symbol and myth with orison and oriflammes. See also René Allendy's ''Paracelsus'' on the birth of the homunculi, Henry Miller, the Glen. This eventful evening in our otherwise prosaic life.''

Again on November 4, 1942, Henry to dinner and in the guest book: ''The important thing tonight is to recall the name of the Latvian or Balkan genius who wrote on the demoniacal artists. Great to know you travelled around the world playing jazz. Bon! Le Jazz Hot! Yes, Larry, to travel around the world is a great joy. Let's learn Mongolian and Urdu. Yours for a good winter. Henry Miller.''

And on Christmas Day, 1942, in the guest book: ''No odes today. Looking forward to a Czechoslovak turkey. Henry Miller.''

April 20, 1943: The other day I gave the ''Quintet'' typescript to Henry Miller to read. On my way home today I stopped by his rooms over the garage at Rose Lodge down canyon. He was nearly through it and very excited—talking enthusiastically for nearly an hour. So all my toil has not gone for naught. Henry believes the book will gain many readers.

April 21, 1943: Saw him again today. Said he thought the book would go like wildfire, would rush in to fill a present vacuum.

April 24, 1943: Henry and neighbors here for dinner last night. Good food and drink and talk, especially by Henry. Kept talking about my story. Said it was like music in writing—which is what I intended it to be. To be to the novel what the string quartet or quintet is to the symphony. He wrote in our guest book: "This time it's a humble admirer, telling you that you've written a fine book—*fine* in the French sense. True, delicate, chaste, sincere, undeniable, and—nostalgic. La vie romantique, vie sensuelle, vie véridique. Je te salue, o frère. Henry Miller 4-23-43."

May 24, 1943: Working here at my desk after dinner with the curtains undrawn when Henry Miller tapped on the door. It elated me to see him. He returned Starkie's book on Rimbaud, and took "Quintet" for a second reading. Henry inscribed my copy of his Capricorn—a Chinese photographic piracy given me by Bill Everson. It belonged to a merchant sailor who went down with his ship in the Atlantic. Henry's visit was a great tonic. The guy radiates a sense of deep integrated purposeful living.

May 30, 1943: This morning Henry Miller returned "Quintet" with a 2,000-word letter to me about it. Very exciting.

June 4, 1943: Just as Everson's response last December gave me the necessary boost to finish the book, so Henry Miller's letter has put the imprimatur on the work. Now I don't give a good goddamn what anyone else says, good or bad. Ten years went into its conception and delivery. It took me all those years to distill its essence from the stuff of my life, to learn what to leave out.

June 14, 1943: Walked down to Henry Miller's the other night about ten o'clock and found him reading in bed—Kirkegaard and Leopardi. Told him how much I liked his review in the *Nation* of Tom Wolfe's Letters to his Mother. Marvelous little essay. Got to talking of writing and had an hour's good exchange.

On June 18 Gordon "Monk" Newell, the sculptor, and Henry Miller came to dinner and Newell read aloud poems by Hopkins, then he and Henry wrote in our guest book:

> Ho the Windhover!
> Monk
> To Christ our Lord—and a little limburger on the side!
> Henry

Later that summer I received the offer from an eastern library fore-seen by Miller. It led to my advancement as director of the UCLA libraries as of January, 1944. The autumn was spent in the war plant; and after commuting a round trip of fifty miles and working eight hours a day, I still had enough drive to commence a long college novel. During lunch hour at work I read Norman Douglas on North Africa and began Elie Faure's monumental history of art, a work passionately recommended by Miller as a veritable aesthetic bible. I have no record of meetings with Miller during that summer and fall of 1943. My life was overflowing with laboring, writing, family, and planning for my new job. On December 10 I ended ten weeks in the plant. In that time I earned $401 or $8.00 a day and wrote 333 pages on the new novel. Then this journal entry:

December 13, 1943: Picked up Henry Miller in the Village and brought him to the canyon. Have seen him only twice the past three months. Things picking up for him. Selling watercolors. Long bitter letter from him in the *New Republic*. Unable to publish his best books in this country.

January 18, 1944: Henry Miller dropped by late Sunday afternoon as I was reading Faure's closing words. I asked him if he had ever called on Faure in Paris. He said no; that several times he had been on the verge of ringing his office bell in the Boulevard St. Germain, when the thought that Faure's medical practice was so busy that he had had time only to write his history of art, so to speak, on his cuff —this thought deterred him, and he never rang, nor did he ever meet Faure. It is a coincidence that Miller should have knocked on my study door just at the moment when I was finishing the set, purchased last July. Henry is getting a miscellany ready for publication, then is going to Monterey for awhile.

Go he did. Over the next fourteen years Miller sent me hundreds of requests for books, all of which the library duly forwarded and all of which were faithfully returned. My periodic visits to him in Big Sur were always restorative. After loading my car with the latest accumulation of letters, periodicals, his books in foreign translation, manuscripts, and typescripts, we would relax at the hot springs down coast a few miles. At the lodge there I played Le Jazz Hot for Henry while he hummed along with my piano. Although he loved music, he was not musical. In the evening we heard Gerhart Muench play Scriabin until even the surf was stilled.

Once when momentarily weary with library administration I threatened to take off for the Closerie des Lilas, or at least the Brasserie Lipp, it was beauteous Eve Miller who urged me to go, whereas Henry, the old Bohemian, was emphatic that I stay. "There aren't many librarians like you," he said. "Guys like me depend on you." So back to the library I went, reconfirmed by his belief.

All that was long ago, when over candlelight supper at Miller's eyrie on Partington Ridge, from which the great cliffs plunged into the Pacific, we recalled that first cold winter in the Côte d'Or and those warmer years in Beverly Glen when our friendship meant the most to both of us.

Seven hundred fifty copies of this book have been designed and printed letterpress from Perpetua types by W. Thomas Taylor in Austin, Texas. An additional one hundred copies are printed on Mohawk Ticonderoga paper, and are signed by the author.